# CALIFORNIA DMV EXAM WORKBOOK

*Challenge the DMV Exam With Confidence: Practice Questions, Detailed Explanations, and Strategies for First-Time Success*

MAX WHEELER

## Table of Contents

**Introduction** ................................................................................................................. 3
   Welcome to your California driver's license journey! ................................................. 3

**Chapter 1: The Basics of Driving in California** ........................................................ 4
   Know the Basic rules of Road. .................................................................................... 4
   Recognizing road signs ............................................................................................... 5
   Drive safely and responsibly ....................................................................................... 8

**Chapter 2: DMV Exam Preparation** ......................................................................... 13
   How to register for the test ........................................................................................ 13
   Effective study strategies .......................................................................................... 14
   Dealing with exam anxiety with confidence ............................................................. 15

**Chapter 3: Interactive Practice Quizzes** ................................................................ 17
   Quiz on road signs and right-of-way rules ................................................................ 17
   Driving rules quiz in specific situations ................................................................... 27
   DMV exam FAQ with detailed explanations ........................................................... 28

**Chapter 4: Safe and Conscious Driving** ................................................................. 46
   Defensive driving and behavior on the road ............................................................. 46
   Dealing with adverse weather conditions ................................................................. 47
   How to avoid distractions behind the wheel ............................................................ 49

**Chapter 5: California-Specific Driving Regulations** .............................................. 52
   Speed limits and parking rules .................................................................................. 52
   California Parking Regulations ................................................................................. 53
   Rules for drivers of commercial vehicles ................................................................. 57
   What to do in case of traffic accidents ...................................................................... 59

**Chapter 6: Comprehensive Practice Tests** ............................................................ 63
   Complete DMV exam simulations ............................................................................ 63
   Evaluate your progress and identify areas for improvement .................................... 83
   Prepare for the exam day: ......................................................................................... 84
   Conclusion ................................................................................................................. 85
   Congratulations, you're ready for the DMV exam! .................................................. 85
   Additional California Driving Safety and Information Resources ........................... 86

**Appendix** .................................................................................................................. 87
   Glossary of driving terminology ............................................................................... 87
   Road sign summary cards ......................................................................................... 89

**Notes and space for personal annotations**..................................................................102

# Introduction

## Welcome to your California driver's license journey!

Congratulations on taking the first step towards becoming a licensed driver in the Golden State. Obtaining your driver's license is an exciting milestone, as it opens up a world of new opportunities and freedom on the road. Whether you're a teenager eager to experience the independence of driving or an adult looking to enhance your mobility, this journey is filled with valuable lessons and experiences that will stay with you for a lifetime.

As you embark on this journey, you'll be equipped with the knowledge and skills necessary to be a responsible and confident driver. Throughout this process, you'll learn about traffic laws, road signs, defensive driving techniques, and essential road etiquette. You'll gain an understanding of the rules and regulations that govern California's roadways, helping you navigate through different driving scenarios with ease and confidence.

Your safety, as well as the safety of others, is our top priority. Remember, driving is not just a privilege; it comes with significant responsibilities. As a licensed driver, you have a crucial role in making our roads safer for everyone. Always abide by traffic laws, drive defensively, and show courtesy and respect to fellow drivers and pedestrians. We encourage you to approach this journey with dedication and a willingness to learn. Take advantage of the resources provided by the DMV, such as study guides, practice exams, and educational materials. These tools will aid you in preparing for the written exam and the behind-the-wheel test.

Throughout your journey, don't hesitate to seek guidance and support from experienced drivers, friends, or family members who can share valuable insights and experiences. And remember, it's okay to feel a little nervous – it's a natural part of the process. Embrace the challenges, stay focused, and you'll find yourself growing into a confident and capable driver.

Your California driver's license is not just a card in your wallet; it represents your commitment to safe and responsible driving. So, as you hit the road to explore this beautiful state, carry with you the principles of safety, courtesy, and responsibility.

Once again, welcome to your California driver's license journey! We wish you the best of luck, and we look forward to celebrating your success as a licensed driver. Drive safely, and may your journey be filled with wonderful experiences and adventures on California's roads.

# Chapter 1: The Basics of Driving in California

## Know the Basic rules of Road.

The following are the top 10 rules in the California Vehicle Code (CVC) that have been shown to reduce the number of accidents involving motor vehicles:

## Turbo Caps:

One of the most common causes of automobile accidents, especially on the motorway, is reckless driving, namely excessive speeding. The conditions of the road (including "weather, visibility, traffic, surface area, and width of the highway") must be considered at all times by drivers, as per CVC Section 22350. State and local governments set the "prima facie" speed limits, which might vary by road type and are sometimes lower than actual posted speeds. CVC 22349 mandates a 65 mph speed limit on most highways and motorways, with the following speeds enforced at highway interchanges and on surface streets: There is a 15 mph speed restriction at all times in alleyways, on highway overpasses, and at train crossings. When approaching or passing a school or elder care facility during school hours, the speed limit is reduced to 25 miles per hour. Unless otherwise specified by local authorities, this restriction also applies to other business and residential areas. CVC 22400(a) makes it illegal to go so slowly as to impede traffic flow, in addition to making it illegal to go too quickly.

## Driving on the right side of the road while passing oncoming traffic:

Head-on collisions, in which one vehicle forces another off the road or causes a swerve, are typically caused by drivers' failure to stay on the right and avoid passing in no-passing zones. CVC 21650 states that, in most situations, drivers must keep to the right side of the road until passing another vehicle (section 21650(a)), making a left turn (section 21650(b)), or driving on the left side of the road due to construction or maintenance (section 21650(c)). It is unlawful to cross double yellow lines except at driveway entrances and designated turn lanes. (CVC 21460(a)).

## Turn signals are required:

Accidents may occur when drivers fail to indicate their turns to other drivers properly. A signal of this kind is required by CVC 22107 and 22018 one hundred feet before the beginning of the deviation to the right or left.

## Safe traffic practices at intersections under the legislation.

Many sections of the California Vehicle Code pertain to roadway crossings and the people who approach, travel through, and turn into them. According to Section 21800, drivers who approach an intersection must give way to oncoming traffic, vehicles that have already entered the intersection, and, in general, the car on the left must give way to the car on the right if the intersection lacks traffic lights or signs. Under Section 21452, a driver will get a warning that a forthcoming red light is imminent. According to Section 21453, all vehicles must come to a complete stop before the limit line as they approach a red, steady circular traffic light. It also prohibits going through an intersection or activating a turn signal while the light is red. California Vehicle Code Section 21802 mandates that all vehicles must stop completely when approaching a stop sign, yield to any vehicles close enough to represent an "immediate hazard," and continue yielding until it is safe to go. After then, the driver is free to go, and the other vehicles must make way for the one approaching or crossing the intersection.

Prohibition Against Following Too Closely: "Tailgating," or following a vehicle too closely behind the one in front of you, is a major cause of motorway accidents and rear-end collisions at intersections on surface streets. When taking into account the speed of the vehicle in front of you, the traffic volume, and the road condition, you should not follow "more closely than is reasonable and prudent," as stated in CVC 21703.

Left turns require the driver to wait until all approaching vehicles are safely out of the way, as with a U-turn across oncoming traffic. Please see CVC 21802. Therefore, the party turning left must yield to traffic coming from the other direction.

Changing lanes on a surface street or highway: CVC 22107 states that vehicles may only veer to the right or left if doing so is safe and after signaling their intent to do so. Dangerous lane changes without signaling, checking the rear and side view mirrors, and altering lanes at the proper moment are leading causes of "sideswipe" accidents, which may cause vehicles (especially motorcycles) to run off the road.

## You are not allowed to stop or park here:
Vehicles, whether occupied or unoccupied, are not permitted to be parked in the following areas: intersections (other than next to the curb), crosswalks, no parking zones denoted by a red painted curb, within 15 feet of a fire station, in front of a public or private driveway, on any portion of a sidewalk, along a street when it obstructs traffic, double parking and adjacent to another vehicle that is already parked. Drivers are prohibited from opening the door of a parked vehicle unless it is safe to do so (Section 22517).

## Driving Under the Influence of Alcohol or Drugs:
Drunk driving is illegal because it compromises a person's ability to operate a vehicle safely.

## Responsibility for Vehicle Maintenance:
All automobiles, trucks, and SUVs must be maintained in roadworthy condition under CVC 26451 and 26453. Turn signals, brake lights, and parking lights are all a part of this system. There are stricter requirements for the upkeep and regular inspection of commercial vehicles. (CVC 2813).

## Ability to Read Traffic Signs
Important information about the road's laws, regulations, and routes is shown on traffic signs. They're not only for decoration; they're alerts and warnings about driving conditions.

Signs are designed using a variety of shapes, colors, and symbols to ensure that everyone can easily read them.

There are many sorts of traffic signs, including:

## Legislative Signs

Regulatory signs remind you of the laws governing traffic and the roads and what you should and should not do when faced with certain traffic circumstances.

Regulation signs are square or rectangular in design and are written or include symbols in black or red on a white background.

**Here are some examples of regulatory signs:**

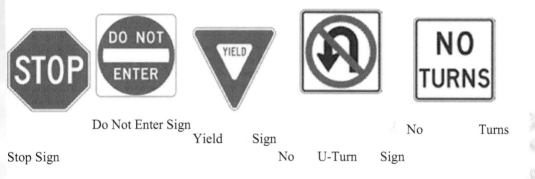

Stop Sign

Do Not Enter Sign

Yield Sign

No U-Turn Sign

No Turns Sign

Stop Sign: a red octagon

Do Not Enter Sign: red circle with a horizontal white stripe through the centre

Yield Sign: yield signs are red on the outside and white in the middle

No U-Turn Sign: white with a black arrow that's crossed out in red

No Turns: white background with a black border and lettering

## Signs of Trouble

The purpose of warning signs is to notify drivers to potential dangers or road conditions ahead.

Yellow diamonds with black wording or symbols are the standard shape for warning signs.

Some potential red flags include the following.

Lane Ends Merge Left (Yellow, diamond-shaped sign)    Signal Ahead    Sharp Right Angle Turn Ahead    Advisory Speed Highway Ramp    Lane Merge

---

A yellow diamond-shaped sign indicates that a lane ends and traffic should merge left.

Warning! Diamond-shaped, yellow sign with a black traffic signal emblem.

Ahead, a yellow diamond-shaped sign with a black right-angle emblem warns of a pending abrupt right-angle bend.

Warning of Increased Speed A speed warning for an exit ramp from a highway is indicated by a yellow, rectangular sign with black letters.

Sign showing a lane merging, with black letters on a yellow rectangle.

## Guide Signs

Guide signs play a vital role in providing essential information about roads, highways, distances, and directions to various destinations.

These signs are typically square or rectangular in shape and feature green or brown backgrounds with white lettering.

Below, I present a selection of guide sign examples:"

Interstate Route Sign    US Route Sign    County Route Sign    Freeway Exit Sign    Highway Guide Sign

---

Interstate Route Sign: Blue shield with red and white lettering.

US Route Sign: Black and white shield with number.

County Route Sign: Square with green background and white lettering.

7

Freeway Exit Sign: Green with white lettering and directional arrows.

Highway Guide Sign: Blue or green with white lettering indicating destinations and distances.

## Temporary Traffic Control Signs:

Temporary traffic control signs are typically neon orange with black writing and are either diamond or square in shape to alert drivers to road maintenance or other temporary road restrictions.

Road Ahead    Work Flagger Sign    Ahead Right Ahead    Lane Closed Ahead    Exit Closed Sign    Detour Sign

Road Work Ahead: Orange with black text, diamond-shaped sign.

Flagger Ahead Sign: Orange with black text, rectangular-shaped sign.

Right Lane Closed Ahead: Orange with black text, diamond-shaped sign.

Exit Closed Sign: Red with white text, rectangular-shaped sign.

Detour Sign: Yellow with black text, diamond-shaped sign.

## Services and Recreation Signs

Various services, such as petrol stations, rest areas, restaurants, campsites, and hospitals, may be located with the help of services signage.

Services signs are square or rectangular, and are blue with white text or symbols.

Some examples of such directions signs are shown below.

Highway Service Sign    Food Highway Service Sign    Gas Hospital Sign    Emergency Medical Services    Highway Rest Area Sign

Highway Food Service Sign: Green with a fork and knife symbol.

Highway Gas Service Sign: Blue with a gas pump symbol.

Hospital Sign: White with a red "H" symbol.

Emergency Medical Services: White with a blue "Star of Life" symbol.

Highway Rest Area Sign: Brown with a picnic table symbol.

**Railroad                         Crossing                         Sign**

Railroad Crossing signs inform you that you are approaching a railroad crossing.

Below are a couple of examples of Railroad Crossing signs:

Railroad Crossing Sign

Railroad Crossing Ahead

Railroad Crossing Sign: Yellow with black "X" shape and two black diagonal lines forming an "X".

Railroad Crossing Ahead: Yellow diamond-shaped sign with black "Railroad Crossing" text and a black "X" symbol.

# Drive safely and responsibly

**Keep an eye on your environment.**

Safe driving requires awareness of your surroundings. The ability to quickly assess and respond to road dangers is greatly enhanced by this.

As for the green, they're one step ahead of you.

In the same room as you.

This blind area is yellow.

The colour red means to look back.

**Examine Your Environment**

Always keep your eyes moving and monitor the road at least 10 seconds ahead of your car to allow yourself time to respond and avoid last-second maneuvers and potential dangers.

(Following too closely or tailgating)
Because the car in front of you restricts your vision, tailgating makes it more difficult to see the road ahead. If the motorist in front of you abruptly stops, you won't have enough time to respond. Observe the three-second rule to maintain a safe following distance and prevent an accident. You have ample time to react if another driver makes a mistake if you follow other cars at a safe distance.

- Take your foot off the gas if a car merges in front of you too closely. This gives the car in front of you some room.
- Make extra room in front of your car.
- There is a tailgater behind you. Keep moving forward at the same pace. When it is safe, move to the right to switch lanes and let the tailgating person pass.
- Following motorcycles over gravel and metal surfaces (such as railroad tracks and bridge gratings).

## Recognize what is on your side.

Take note of what is around you on either side. To keep adequate room for safe maneuvers and to respond to other drivers:
Keep out of other driver's blind spots and steer clear of following closely behind them.
Even if you have the right-of-way, provide room for cars entering highways. Be prepared for sudden shifts and watch for other drivers' signals.
Keep a safe distance between your car and any parked cars, and always look both ways when approaching intersections with a stop sign or red light.
There are blind zones in every car. When gazing straight ahead or in the mirrors, a motorist cannot see these regions surrounding the vehicle. The blind spots for most automobiles are to the sides and somewhat to the driver's back.
Look out of your side windows to your right and left over your shoulders to check your blind spots. You should tilt your head to look. Avoid turning the steering wheel or your whole body. Before you: Look for blind spots.
• Alternate lanes.
• At an intersection, turn.
• Join the traffic.
• Go back.
• Reserve a spot for parking.
• Park parallel.
• Back up to the curb.
• Unlock the automobile door.
• Your blind spots are in the darkened regions.

## Recognize what is behind you.

By being aware of your surroundings, you may prevent rear-end crashes. Utilizing your side mirrors and rearview mirror, and moving your head, often check for vehicles behind you:
• Alternate lanes.
• Look out for blind areas.
• Go more slowly.

- Enter a driveway or side street.
- Slow down before entering a parking place.
- Approach the curb and back away from it.
- Go back.

## Recognizing the Condition of the roads

## Darkness

Ensure you can stop in the area illuminated by your headlights while driving at night. When feasible, use your high-beam headlights. This includes wide-open spaces and pitch-black metropolitan streets. If using high beams is prohibited anywhere, don't do it. To prevent blinding an approaching car, turn down your bright beams. If the lights of another vehicle are too intense:
- Avoid staring into the path of approaching headlights.
- Keep an eye on the lane's right edge.
- Keep a peripheral eye out for the approaching car.
- Avoid turning on your high beams in response to the other motorist. This merely makes it more difficult for you both to see.

## Skids

When one or more tires cannot contact the pavement, a skid occurs, and the car slides. Your vehicle may need help to control. There are several kinds of skids.

## Skid-resistant Surfaces

Your car may slide if there is ice or compacted snow on the road. If you are moving too quickly or downhill, this is considerably more likely to happen. Maintain a safe distance between your car and the one in front of you when driving slowly. To avoid stumbling on slick surfaces:
- Be cautious while approaching bends and junctions. Slow down as you approach and navigate steep turns.
- Steer clear of sudden stops and twists.
- Before traveling down a steep slope, go into low gear.
- Keep away from places where there is ice, oil, damp leaves, or standing water.

**If you begin to skid, do these actions:**
1. Gradually take your foot off the gas pedal.
2. Avoid using the brakes.
3. Rotate the steering wheel towards the skid's direction.
4. Attempt to place a wheel on a dry surface.
5. Police Traffic Infractions

The policeman gently moves across lanes while turning on their emergency lights. Traffic pauses are used by law enforcement to:
- Reduce or halt traffic to clear the route of dangers.
- In times of dense fog or other exceptional traffic conditions, vehicles should slow down or halt.

- Avoid crashes in odd circumstances.

## You ought to:

- Flash your emergency lights to alert other motorists.
- Slowly reduce your pace to match that of the police. Except when it's essential to prevent an accident, avoid abrupt braking. Keep a safe gap between you and the police car in front of you.
- Do not pass the police car. Please wait until the officer switches off their emergency lights and the traffic situation permits you to resume traveling at your regular pace before accelerating.

## Questions with Multiple Choices:

1. According to the California Vehicle Code (CVC), what is one of the most frequent reasons for car accidents, particularly those involving freeways?

A) failing to indicate turns correctly
B) tailgating
C) operating a vehicle while intoxicated or high
D) exceeding legal speed restrictions

2. What contributes most to head-on crashes, car runs off the road, and swerving situations?

A) failing to drive on the correct side of the road
B) hazardous lane changes
C) failing to surrender the right of way
D) operating a vehicle when intoxicated or otherwise impaired

3. According to the California Vehicle Code (CVC), how long ahead should you indicate a turn intention?

a) 50 feet  b) 100 feet  c) 200 feet  d) 500 feet.

4. What kind of traffic sign informs drivers where different facilities—including gas stations, rest areas, and hospitals—are located?

A. a) Regulation signs
B. b) Warning signs
C. c) Directions signs
D. Temporary traffic control signs

5. Before changing lanes, what should you do to check your blind spots?

A. Use your side mirrors and rearview mirror.
B. Peer out of your side windows.
C. Rely only on your side mirrors
D. Completely turn your body and the steering wheel

6. How can you avoid skidding on slick surfaces like ice and packed snow?

A) Aim to drive gently and give other drivers room to pass.

B) Use your brakes to slow down as you approach junctions and bends
C) Make rapid turns and stops to stay in control.
D) Change into high gear before descending a steep hill.

7. What should you do if you encounter a traffic stop by law police on the road? To prevent delays, you should either:
   A. Pass the police car swiftly.
   B. Please slow down and keep a safe distance from it.
   C. Ignore the patrol car and keep going at your current pace.
   D. Use your emergency lights to alert the officer.

# Answer Key:

1. D)
2. A)
3. B)
4. C)
5. B)
6. A)
7. B)

# Chapter 2: DMV Exam Preparation

## How to register for the test
Follow the following steps to register in DMV exam.

**Verify Your Eligibility:** Confirm that you are qualified to take the test before enrolling. You must be a specific age (typically 16 or older) and fulfill any other criteria imposed by your state's DMV.

**Collect the necessary documents:** Gather the evidence to confirm your eligibility, residence, and identity. These papers often include your identity (such as a current passport or birth certificate), social security number, and evidence of habitation (utility bills, a lease agreement, etc.).

Get a copy of the driver's manual or handbook issued by the DMV in your state and read it. You need to know the material in this handbook on traffic signs, driving laws, and road regulations to pass the test.

**Select the kind of exam:** Decide whether you will be taking a written knowledge test or a hybrid written and practical driving test. Online knowledge tests may also be available in certain states.
The test. You may do this by phoning the DMV office or doing it online.

## Fee for the Exam:
Pay the fee for the exams.

**Make an Appointment:** Depending on the DMV regulations in your state, you may need to make an appointment to register for the test and pay the necessary exam cost. The price could change depending on the kind of test you're taking.

**Attend the Exam:** Show up at the DMV office or the appropriate exam site at a specified time and day. Bring all necessary documentation, such as a valid form of identification and your registration confirmation.

**Take the Test:** Multiple-choice questions based on the content in the driver's handbook often make up the written knowledge test. Select the best response after carefully reading the questions. If you take a practical driving test, be prepared to display your driving abilities.

**Get Results:** Your exam results will be sent to you after completion. Depending on the laws in your state, if you pass the test, you can be granted a learner's permit or a driver's license. If you don't pass, ask the DMV about the retake policy and any prerequisites or waiting periods that could be required.

**Experience and Acquire Experience:** Once you get your learner's permit, utilize it to get some experience behind the wheel while closely supervised by a certified adult. To prepare for your driving test, practice and learn the traffic laws.

Remember to study hard, practice defensive driving, and show confidence before taking the DMV test. Your chances of passing the test and receiving your driver's license will rise if you are well-prepared.

# Effective study strategies

You may demonstrate that you understand traffic rules and safety regulations by receiving a California driver's license knowledge exam score of at least 38 out of 46. Contrary to myths, these tests are not intended to deceive novice drivers. All of the quiz questions are based on the California Driver Handbook. You boost your chances of passing and decrease your stress levels when you thoroughly study and prepare.

### Tips for the Written Driving Test in Studying
Use the following study techniques to be ready for the written portion of the California DMV driving test:

### Put the value of driver's education first.
You may prepare for the written portion of the driving exam by taking a driver education course. You may finish it at your leisure since it's online. You may evaluate your understanding of the material and determine if you are prepared to take the DMV exam by using the provided sample exams. You don't need to go anywhere to take the easy and reasonably priced online course!

### Examine the manual and take practice exams.

Thoroughly read the California Driver Handbook, make notes, and give explanations for any terminology that could be more apparent. Make sure you comprehend all of the ideas and regulations. If you need clarification, you may mark certain passages and do an internet study or see a specialist. Even watching movies online might help you recall concepts and ideas more clearly.
The California DMV provides example driver license knowledge practice examinations, much as in your driver's education course. Please familiarize yourself with the language and format of the written test by reviewing these. Every time you take a practice exam, evaluate your progress and identify the areas that need additional in-depth study.

Education concept: handing out exercise tests to students and having them complete exam carbon paper computer sheets.

## Practice your test-taking techniques.

Make sure to relax and get a good night's sleep the night before your exam. Eat a healthy meal the morning before, and listen to uplifting music while you go to the DMV. Examine each question thoroughly, emphasizing crucial phrases as necessary. Use the process of elimination to attempt to reduce your decision to the top two options if you are unsure about an answer. When selecting the right response, use common sense. Last but not least, verify your work again in case you still need to look at something.

## Understand what you must bring.

Teenagers between the ages of 15.5 and 18 must obtain several documentation before taking the vision and writing tests. These include a completed application for a driver's license, an original birth certificate, evidence that you finished driver's ed, a document with your social security number, proof of your identification and legal status in the United States, and documentation of your domicile in California.

The DMV clerk will take the young driver's fingerprints and a picture once they have submitted these documents, had a vision examination and passed a knowledge test. Please be aware that for the first year after receiving your permit, you are not permitted to drive between the hours of 11 p.m. and 5 a.m. or to transport anyone under the age of 20 unless you are accompanied by a parent, legal guardian, licensed driver over the age of 25, or qualified driving instructor.

Keep an optimistic outlook and positive thoughts regarding the written portion of the California DMV driving test. In addition, you only need to pay for a fresh application after the first three attempts at the exam. If you don't pass, you must wait a week before trying again.

## Last Words on Preparing for Your DMV Exam

Only walk-ins are permitted for knowledge examinations, although it is recommended that you take the test in the morning when your mind is fresh and prepared to tackle the problems.

Contact Alliance Defensive Driving School professionals to learn more about the study techniques that can help you pass the written CA DMV test. Our qualified specialists will gladly answer any inquiries you have.

# Dealing with exam anxiety with confidence

It's normal to have anxiety or worry when getting ready for an exam, particularly the California DMV permit test. However, you may overcome your fear and improve your exam-passing prospects using excellent study techniques. How to prepare for your DMV exam is as follows:

**Study carefully:** Study the California Driver Handbook to eliminate uncertainties and worries that cause tension. You'll feel more certain on exam day the more you study. Use practice exams like the Marathon Test and Exam Simulator to strengthen your understanding and boost your confidence.

**Manage Your Time:** To ensure you have enough time to cover all the content, plan your study program before the exam date. Avoid cramming the night before since it might make you more stressed.

**Techniques for Distraction:** If you find that worrying about the test makes you more nervous, use distraction techniques on the day of the test. Take part in enjoyable activities, such as hobbies, domestic duties done while listening to music, or running errands.

**Keep Calm:** On the other side, if being busy makes you feel more nervous, choose soothing pursuits like yoga, meditation, or quiet reading. To unwind before the exam, think about rewarding yourself with a massage.

**Seek Support:** Surround yourself with friends, family, or other close relatives who can cheer you on and assist you in getting ready. They may test you and give you more self-assurance.

**Planning:** Review the content the night before the exam and avoid tiresome pursuits like binge-watching TV or drinking too much alcohol. To guarantee you are well-rested for the test, get a good night's sleep.

**Start Your Day Off Right:** Eat a healthy meal the morning before the exam and do some moderate exercise to keep your mind sharp. Avoid stressful circumstances and concentrate on having positive test-passing ideas.

Just remember that thorough research and preparation can boost your self-assurance and assist you in overcoming permit exam nervousness. Believe that you can succeed and see yourself passing the exam. Using these techniques, you may go into the DMV permit exam with a winning attitude and raise your chances of passing. Good fortune!

# Chapter 3: Interactive Practice Quizzes

## Quiz on road signs and right-of-way rules

### Test Quizz 1

Which of the following signs represents two-way traffic?

1. This sign warns you about

   Yellow diamond shape with black symbol

   a) Road Work Ahead

   b) No U-Turn

   c) Slippery Road

   d) Pedestrian Crossing

2. The broken white lines on the pavement mean that

   a) Passing is allowed

   b) No passing is allowed

   c) Yield to oncoming traffic

   d) Merge with traffic

3. What type of sign is this?

   Yellow and round with a black "X" and two intersecting black lines forming an "R" shape.

a) Regulatory Sign

b) Warning Sign

c) Guide Sign

d) Railroad Crossing Sign

4. What does this sign mean?
   Color: Usually white (symbol) and black (text) on a blue background.
   Shape: Rectangular with rounded corners.

a) School Zone Ahead

b) No Parking Zone

c) Pedestrian Crossing

d) Watch for Bicycles

5. What does this regulatory sign mean?
   Color: Usually black and white.

   Shape: Rectangular.

a) Speed Limit Ahead

b) No Right Turn

c) No Left Turn

d) No Stopping or Standing

6. This sign represents
   Green rectangle with white text.

a) Hospital Ahead

b) Highway Exit

c) Rest Area

d) Gas Station Ahead

7. This warning sign represents
   Yellow with a downward-pointing triangle.

a) Low Clearance

b) Road Work Ahead

c) Slippery When Wet

d) Watch for Deer

8. What does this warning sign mean?

Rectangular with a black background and white arrow

a) Do Not Enter

b) No U-Turn

c) One Way Traffic

d) Steep Hill Ahead

9. When you come near an intersection with a through road but without stop signs or yield signs, you should

 a) Reduce your speed and continue with care

b) Halt and wait for the traffic signal to become green

c) Halt and give way to all traffic on the through road d) Accelerate to clear the intersection swiftly

10. A consistent red arrow indication indicates

a) Proceed with care

b) Halt and give way to approaching vehicles

c) Execute a right turn

d) Refrain from executing the motion depicted by the arrow

11. At a crosswalk without any markings, you should

a) Reduce your speed and proceed with care

b) Come to a halt and give way to pedestrians

c) Honk your horn to notify pedestrians

d) Continue without stopping if there are no pedestrians visible

12. If all the back seats are presently taken by kids below 7 years old, a child below 8 years old has the option to:

a) Occupy the front seat while wearing a seatbelt

b) Occupy the front seat solely if the vehicle is equipped with airbags

c) Refrain from occupying the front seat

d) Occupy the front seat solely if the child is at least 4 feet 9 inches in height

Solution:

1. c) 2. a) 3. d) 4. c) 5. a) 6. b) 7. a) 8. d) 9. a) 10. d) 11. b) 12. c)

# QUIZZ 2

1. If the arrow at a traffic signal is flashing yellow, you are required to: a) remain stationary until the light changes to green, b) give right of way to approaching vehicles and pedestrians, c) Execute a U-turn if it can be done safely d) Perform an immediate left turn without coming to a halt

2. If the arrow at a traffic signal is flickering yellow, you ought to:

a) remain until the light transforms into a green

b) give priority to approaching vehicles and pedestrians

c) execute a U-turn if it is secure to proceed

d) make a left turn without coming to a halt.

3. At a junction, who is privileged when the signal changes to green if you and a bicyclist are getting ready to make a right turn?

a) The cyclist has the privilege of passage. b) You have permission to go ahead.

c) You and the bicycle can proceed simultaneously. d) The pedestrian is entitled to priority.

4. Which automobile has the privilege of passage when two vehicles encounter each other on a narrow mountain pathway, and neither can overtake?

a) The vehicle ascending the hill is granted the privilege of passage. b) The vehicle descending the hill is granted the privilege of passage.

c) The vehicle with the larger engine size has priority on the road. d) The quicker vehicle is granted permission to proceed at an intersection.

5. Without any other instructions, the highest lawful velocity for automobiles towing trailers on a two-lane non-separated road is _____.

a) 55 miles per hour

b) 65 miles per hour

c) 45 miles per hour

d) 50 miles per hour

6. When you observe farm animals close to the road, you should: a) sound your horn to startle the livestock aside

b) reduce your speed and proceed with care

c) accelerate to overtake them quickly

d) disregard them and continue driving at your usual speed upon spotting them near the highway.

7. Reversible lanes, HOV lanes, bicycle lanes, and road dividers are all instances of the significance behind double yellow lines spaced every two feet. On a two-way road, the "turnout" sections

a) are for executing U-turns

b) are for weary drivers

c) are spots to pull over and unwind

d) are spots to halt and appreciate the scenery.

8. Right turns on red lights are allowed only when:

a) coming from a single-direction road into another single-direction road

b) there is no oncoming traffic or pedestrians

c) the red arrow signal is blinking

d) in no situation.

9. If you are disabled and have a placard, use the ___ colored curb.

a) Curb painted in blue b) Curb painted in red c) Curb painted in yellow d) Curb painted in green

10. Which of the subsequent options is not a shade of green? It is a minor offense that can result in

a) a monetary penalty

b) participation in community work

c) temporary revocation of a license

d) confinement

11. For anyone who escapes or attempts to avoid law enforcement officers involved in the execution of their duties, they should adhere to:

a) Rule of Three Seconds b) Rule of One Second c) Rule of Five Seconds d) Rule of Ten Seconds

12. If you desire to avoid tailgating, utilize your:

a) Bright headlights b) Hazard lights c) Dim headlights d) Fog lights if you need to drive in fog.

13. Upon perceiving the siren of an emergency vehicle, you ought to either:

a) Decelerate and continue moving through the intersection. b) Perform a 180-degree turn and proceed in the opposite direction.

c) Proceed directly through the intersection and stop on the right side. d) Speed through the junction and exit it as quickly as possible.

14. When you observe a truck with a cautionary symbol, you should presume that the contents within could be dangerous.

a) Orange triangle

b) Blue rectangle

c) Red octagon

d) Green circle

15. Hydroplaning refers to a lack of command while operating a vehicle and can be prevented by either:

a) abruptly applying the brakes to regain control

b) forcefully turning the steering wheel in the opposite direction. c) reducing the throttle and steering towards the desired direction d) increasing acceleration to gain traction.

| Answer Key: | |
|---|---|
| | 1. b) |

| 2. c) | 3. a) |
|---|---|
| 4. a) | 5. c) |
| 6. b) | 7. d) |
| 8. a) | 9. Red painted curb |
| 10. c) | 11. d) |
| 12. a) | 13. c) |
| 14. a) | **15.** c) |

## Test Quizz 3

1. The most common causes of locked wheels in skids are
(1) quick acceleration
(2) heavy braking
(3) Excessive steering during a curve
(4) Under-inflated tyres

2. if your parked car rolls into an unattended one, you should either: a) wait for the other car's owner to return and take responsibility for the accident
 b) leave a note on the other car with your contact information; c) report the incident to the police right away
 d) drive away without taking responsibility for the accident.

3. If the accident is serious, the motorist has to report it to the DMV.
a) 10 days
b) 15 days
c) 20 days
d) 30 days

**True statement on lane markings:** Two parallel solid yellow lines enable passing with caution; a solid yellow line and a dashed white line indicate regions where passing is permitted; a double solid yellow line indicates restricted areas.

5. Turn on your headlights no later than _____ after dark.
 time in minutes:
a) fifteen
 b) thirty
c) one-hour
d) one and a half hours

When stopped by law enforcement, what should you do first?
A) Remain seated in the driver's seat with your hands on the wheel
B) Get out of the car and talk to the cop
C) Turn off the car's engine and stay still
D) Call for help from a friend or family membe.

7 A passenger car traveling at 55 mph may stop at a safe distance of
a) 100 feet
b) 200 feet
c) 300 feet
d) 400 feet under ideal circumstances.

An upward-pointing hand and arm from a motorist in front of you mean they want to either:
a) turn left
b) turn right
c) slow down or stop
d) do a U-turn.

8. A pair of parallel white lines:
a) It divides one way of traffic from the other
b) It permits passing when it is safe
c) It indicates a turn lane
d) It forbids switching lanes.

9. A full stop and waiting for an opening in traffic
A. Signal, accelerate, and merge into traffic when it is safe to do so
B. Horn honking to notify other vehicles
C. Driving in the breakdown lane until a gap in traffic occurs is option D.

Answer Key:

| 1. b) | 2. b) |
| 3. a) | 4. a) |
| 5. b) | 6. a) |
| 7. c) | 8. c) |
| 9. d) | |

# Driving rules quiz in specific situations

## Test quizz 4

Question 1: How can you prevent blinding the driver of an oncoming vehicle when driving at night with your high-beam headlights?

A) Use high-beam lights in areas where they are not prohibited.

B) Keep your high-beam headlights on and signal the other driver to lower their beams.

C) Adjust your high-beam headlights to avoid dazzling the driver coming towards you.

D) Stare directly into the oncoming headlights to signal the other driver.

Question 2: What measures can you take to avoid skidding on slippery surfaces like ice or compacted snow?

A) Drive at high speeds to maintain traction on slippery surfaces.

B) Downshift to low gear after descending a steep hill on a slippery surface.

C) Refrain from making sharp turns and sudden stops on slippery surfaces.

D) Reduce the distance between your vehicle and the one ahead when driving on slippery surfaces.

Question 3: If your vehicle starts to skid, what is the appropriate action to take?

A) Apply the brakes forcefully to regain control of the vehicle.

B) Turn the steering wheel towards the direction of the skid.

C) Shift to a higher gear to stabilize the vehicle.

D) Gradually release your foot from the accelerator and turn the steering wheel in the direction of the skid.

Question 4: What is the primary purpose of a Law Enforcement Traffic Break?

A) To allow law enforcement officers to take a rest during their duty hours.

B) To deliberately cause traffic congestion in abnormal traffic conditions.

C) To stop traffic and issue citations to all drivers on the road.

D) To slow down or halt traffic in order to remove hazards from the road or prevent collisions during unusual traffic conditions.

Question 5: How should you respond when encountering a Law Enforcement Traffic Break?

A) Speed up and swiftly pass the patrol vehicle to avoid any delays.

B) Activate your emergency flashers and maintain your current speed.

C) Gradually reduce your speed to match the speed of the officer and keep a safe distance from the patrol vehicle ahead of you.

D) Suddenly brake to alert other drivers about the traffic break.

Answer key:

1. C) Adjust your high-beam headlights to avoid dazzling the driver coming towards you.
2. C) Refrain from making sharp turns and sudden stops on slippery surfaces.
3. D) Gradually release your foot from the accelerator and turn the steering wheel in the direction of the skid.
4. D) To slow down or halt traffic in order to remove hazards from the road or prevent collisions during unusual traffic conditions.

5. C) Gradually reduce your speed to match the speed of the officer and keep a safe distance from the patrol vehicle ahead of you.

# DMV exam FAQ with detailed explanations

## Test quizz 5

1. Are there any circumstances where it is permissible to veer off the designated road while passing another vehicle?

    A) If your vehicle can fit comfortably within the width of the shoulder. B) In the event that the car in front of you decides to make a left turn. C) Always in every situation.

2. As you draw near to an unregulated railway intersection with restricted visibility, your line of sight is obstructed, preventing you from observing a distance of 400 feet along the tracks in a single direction. What is the maximum velocity allowed?
    a. 10 mph. B) 20 mph. C) 25 mph. D) 15 mph.

3. When manoeuvring your car into a parallel parking spot on a flat road, what precautions should you take regarding your wheels?

    A) Make sure your front tyres are facing the road.
    B) Ensure that one of your back tyres is in contact with the curb.
    C) The distance between your wheels and the curb should not exceed 18 inches.

4. What is the appropriate way to modify your speed when entering the motorway?

    A) Maintain a speed that is 5 to 10 MPH below the average speed of vehicles on the motorway.
    B) Adhere to the designated velocity restriction for vehicles on the motorway.
    C) Keep pace with the flow of vehicles on the motorway.

5. What lights should be used while driving in fog?

    A) Exclusively fog lamps. B) Bright headlights. B) Dim headlights.

6. What is the meaning of a curb that has been painted white?

    A) Area designated for the loading and unloading of cargo or individuals.
    B) Restricted area for individuals or packages exclusively.
    C) Exclusive area for the transportation of cargo.

7. As you're driving, you notice a school bus ahead of you, its red lights flashing. What actions are recommended?

        A) Halt, and continue once you believe all the kids have disembarked from the vehicle.
        B) Decrease your velocity to 25 miles per hour and overtake with caution.
        C) Cease movement when the red lights are flickering.

8. Can you explain the meaning of California's "Basic Speed Law"?

        A) It is imperative that you never exceed the speed limits indicated on the road signs.
        B) It is important to always maintain a safe driving speed that is appropriate for the present circumstances.
        C) Certain motorways in California have a maximum speed limit of 70 mph.

9. What is the period for notifying the DMV following the sale of your vehicle?
A) an entire week.
B) ten days.
C) Fourteen days.
D) It will require 20 days.

10. What is the suggested range to foresee forthcoming actions and avert abrupt manoeuvres?
A) It requires roughly 5 to 10 seconds.
B) Roughly 10 to 15 seconds
C) Roughly 15 to 20 seconds

11. What is the suggested distance to indicate consistently before executing a left turn?
A) The measurement is 50 feet.
B) The measurement is 75 feet.
C) The measurement is 100 feet.

12. Can it be deemed precise to affirm that all subsequent assertions concerning obscured areas are correct?
A) If there is a reflection on both sides of the vehicle, it will not be taken away.
B) The majority of passenger vehicles possess lesser areas of limited visibility in comparison to big trucks.
C) Rearview mirrors are beneficial for inspecting areas of limited visibility.

13. You discover yourself in a circumstance where you unintentionally collided with an immobile vehicle, but regrettably, the proprietor is nowhere to be located. What activities are suggested?
A) Affix a note to the vehicle.
B) Promptly inform the nearby law enforcement authorities without delay regarding the occurrence, either by getting in touch with the city police department or, in regions without city jurisdiction, by reaching out to the California Highway Patrol (CHP).
C) comprises both of the options mentioned above.

14. What is the typical top speed permitted in a residential area without any explicit indications to the contrary?
A) 20 miles per hour. B) 25 miles per hour. C) 30 miles per hour.

15. What are the particular circumstances in which it is acceptable to impede a junction within the boundaries of the legislation?
A) As you advanced through the intersection while the traffic signal was showing a green light.
B) During the peak of rush hour.
C) By no means.
16. What is the accurate method to align your front wheels when parking uphill on a two-way street lacking a curb?
A) Moved in the contrary direction (facing the street).
B) Turned to the left (in the opposite direction of the road).
C) In sync with the earth's surface.
17. What kinds of automobiles can drivers with a Class C license operate?
A) A tricycle car as long as the vehicle's overall weight does not surpass 6,000 pounds.
B) Any automobile with three axles, irrespective of its mass.
C) A car transporting a couple of trailers.
When initiating your turn from a one-way street with multiple lanes onto another one-way street, which lane should you select to commence your turn?
A) Whatever route (as long as it is safe).
B) The lane next to the pavement on the right.
C) The walkway is situated in the center of the road.
When must you submit a documented statement (SR1) to the Department of Motor Vehicles following a collision?
A) In the case of harm to you or the other motorist.
B) If there is property damage that surpasses $1,000 or the happening of any injuries.
C) Only if you are accountable.
What is the time when road surfaces become the most dangerous because of slippery conditions?
B) During a downpour.
B) Once the precipitation has been descending for a prolonged duration.
C) The first rainfall after a period of dryness.
21. Where are the places where you cannot park your vehicle?
A) Besides the motorway during an emergency.
B) Next to a scarlet-hued curb.
C) In the near vicinity of an elementary school.
22. What is the period for notifying the DMV if you partake in any subsequent activities?
A) Get rid of or transport your vehicle.
B) Fail to meet the requirements of an emissions test for your vehicle.
C) Acquire a new prescription for spectacles or corrective lenses.
21. What actions are advised when coming across two solid, dual, and yellow parallel lines with two or greater feet gap between them?
A) Utilise them to enter or exit a private parking space.
B) Refrain from inciting them in any situation.
C) Consider them as a separate pathway for vehicles.
22. You are keen on turning right at an upcoming intersection. What activities are suggested?

A) Relax and move towards the right side of your lane.
B) Avoid utilizing the bicycle lane for driving.
C) Express your desire to change direction by signaling for a span of 100 feet before executing the turn.

The velocity restriction on the motorway you are presently journeying on is established at 65 miles per hour. The automobiles are traveling at a velocity of 70 miles per hour. What is the maximum allowable speed at which one can legally drive a car?

A) To keep up with the speed of other vehicles on the road, sustaining a velocity of at least 70 miles per hour or above is essential.
B) Within the span of 65 mph to 70 mph.
C) Top speed restriction of 65 mph.

9. In which locations is it against the law to park your automobile?
A) In a non-designated pedestrian crossing.
B) Near a personal driveway.
C) On a cycle path.

10. What is the most secure measure you can adopt concerning using mobile phones and operating a vehicle?
A) Utilising hands-free gadgets to ensure both hands remain on the steering wheel.
B) Ensuring your phone is readily accessible to avoid diverting your gaze from the road.
C) Evaluating the digits before responding to a phone call.

11. You have a signal to proceed, but congestion obstructs the crossing. What actions should you take?
A) Avoid entering the intersection until the traffic subsides.
B) Proceed into the crossroads and remain stationary until the flow of vehicles subsides.
C) Combine with a different lane and maneuver past the congestion.

12. What actions are necessary when preparing to execute a right turn?
A) Indicate and make a prompt maneuver.
B) Indicate and make a prompt maneuver.
C) Decelerate or halt, if needed, and then execute the maneuver.

13. When should you adhere to directions from school crossing monitors?
A) Always.
B) Solely within the designated hours of the educational institution.
C) Except if you do not observe any kids present.

1. Where are the areas where parking your vehicle is not allowed? 10. In what regions is it illegal to abandon your vehicle parked?
A) Strolling across the road without any apparent signs.
B) In near vicinity to an individual's driveway.
C) Cycling within a specified zone for bicycles.

2. What steps can you take to guarantee utmost security when utilizing cell phones while operating a vehicle?
A) Using hands-off technology to guarantee both hands stay on the steering wheel.
B) Making sure your mobile device is easily reachable, removing the necessity to shift your focus away from the road.

C) Verifying the numbers before answering a phone call.
3. Despite the signal indicating to proceed, the crossroad is crowded due to the substantial flow of vehicles. What activities are suggested?
A) Hold off until the road is empty before proceeding into the intersection.
B) Move towards the intersection and stay still until the stream of cars decreases.
C) Merge with an alternate lane and try to circumvent the traffic.
4. What measures should be implemented before carrying out a right turn?
A) Signal and execute a quick maneuver.
B) Signal and execute a quick maneuver.
C) Decrease velocity or stop, if necessary, and then perform the maneuver.
5. When should an individual comply with the instructions provided by school crossing monitors?
A) Always.
B) Solely during the specified period of educational institution functioning.
C) As long as no kids are apparent.

1. What actions should be taken when encountering a sandstorm on a breezy day while driving on the motorway with restricted sight?
A) Brighten up your indoor lighting.
B) Activate your parking lights.
C) Turn on your headlights.
2. What is the optimal approach to utilize when contemplating overtaking another vehicle?
A) Avoid assuming that the other driver will automatically create space for you to rejoin your lane.
B) Assume that the driver in front will allow you to pass once you activate your turn signal.
C) Assume that the other drivers will maintain a steady speed.
3. Thirty-three. While you travel down the highway, the highest velocity permitted is 65 miles per hour. However, most other vehicles are racing along at velocities of 70 miles per hour or even greater. What is the maximum speed that is allowed for driving within the boundaries of the law?
A) Move at a velocity of 70 mph or greater to maintain pace with the movement of automobiles.
B) Within 65 mph to 70 mph
C) Uppermost velocity restriction of 65 mph.
4. What are the possible outcomes of regularly surpassing the speed limit and passing other vehicles on a single-lane road?
A) Your arrival at your desired destination will be accelerated and improved in terms of security.
B) The likelihood of an accident happening will be greater.
C) Your help is vital in reducing the problem of traffic jams.
5. What kinds of automobiles must stop before crossing railway tracks?
A) Motorhomes or trucks towing a trailer for personal watercraft.
B) Caution indicators on tanker vehicles.
C) Any vehicle with three or more axles or a weight surpassing 4,000 pounds.

6. What conditions can you perform a left turn onto another one-way road while driving a vehicle on a one-way street?
A) When a sign indicates clear permission.
B) As automobiles on the street move toward the right side.
C) As automobiles on the street move toward the left side.

While driving, you discover you are following a colossal truck. Abruptly, the truck swerves to the right, getting ready to take a turn onto a busy road with two lanes traveling in both ways. What measures should be implemented by the truck?
A) It possesses the choice to execute its maneuver in either of the two lanes.
B) Adopting a broader trajectory to maneuver toward the right effectively could be essential.
C) It is essential to remain in the appropriate lane when executing a turn consistently.

8. When can another vehicle be passed by crossing a dual yellow line?
A) If there is an uninterrupted marking on the other side of the street.
B) If the marking on your side of the street is impaired.
C) If the other side of the road has a cross marking.

9. What is the appropriate conduct when using a carpool lane?
A) Complying with the designated areas for entering and exiting is crucial.
B) It is crucial to always adhere to traffic laws and guidelines.
C )Refrain from traversing the dual yellow line unless it is imperative for entering or exiting a designated region.
D) Journey at the utmost allowable velocity on the motorway.

10. While engaging in defensive driving
A) upholding a secure gap of at least one automobile span between your vehicle and the one preceding you is crucial.
B) Sustaining an unwavering stare on the automobile in front while maneuvering a motorized vehicle.
C) Consistently surveying your environment to identify potential hazards.

11. What is the suggested method when trailing a large truck on the motorway?
A) Keep a secure distance in adverse weather conditions to improve visibility.
B) Maintaining a greater distance between your vehicle and the one ahead of you is more crucial than a typical car.
C) Keep a secure distance from the truck to guarantee clear visibility.

12. What are some instances of pursuits that are both dangerous and violate the law while driving a vehicle?
A) Shuffling the placement of your side mirrors.
B) Delighting in the harmonious melodies while wearing headphones that cover both ears.
C) Transporting an unrestrained animal inside the vehicle.

13. What situations necessitate you to come to a total stop when nearing railway tracks?
A) If you are incapable of completely journeying to the contrary extremity.
B) Urban regions with consistent train movement where the crossing is situated.
C) If there are several young kids in the vehicle.

14. Driving near another vehicle:
A)May annoy fellow drivers and provoke anger.
B) Won't result in a traffic citation.

C) Aids in mitigating the issue of traffic gridlock.

15. Is it obligatory to always uphold a reduced velocity compared to the other vehicles on the road?

A) Indeed, operating a vehicle at a significantly reduced speed can hinder the seamless traffic flow.
B) Undoubtedly, it is a successful approach for upholding road security.
C) it is always safer to maintain a lower speed than the surrounding traffic.

16. Who is accountable for providing instructions at a road construction location that you must adhere to?

A) The existence of orange cones on the road ahead is the sole indication.
B) Provided they do not conflict with existing indications, cues, or rules.
C) Continuously.

16. What are the regulations for operating in a bicycle lane?

A) When no bicyclists are around, peak-hour traffic can be very heavy.
B) As you get closer to a junction that is within a distance of 200 feet from where you are
C) you plan to execute a turn to the right.
If you require to pass a motorist who is executing a right-hand maneuver.

18. A flashing yellow traffic light at an upcoming intersection indicates:

A) If it is considered safe, stop before entering the junction.
B) Stop and yield to any vehicles from other directions before continuing through the intersection.
C) Decrease your velocity and cautiously maneuver through the intersection.

19. What is the suitable course of action if a pedestrian is traversing your lane ahead and there is no pedestrian crossing?

A) Gaze directly into the pedestrian's gaze before moving ahead.
B) Decrease your velocity as you near the individual strolling.
C) Stop and allow the pedestrian to finish their trip across the street.

20. A continuous yellow line next to a dashed yellow line signifies that vehicles:

A) In both directions are allowed to pass.
B) Next to the dotted line, vehicles are allowed to continue.
C) Automobiles are allowed to pass beside the continuous queue.

1. **Answer key:**

| 2.  C)   | 3.  A)  |
|----------|---------|
| 4.  C)   | 5.  B)  |
| 6.  B)   | 7.  A)  |
| 8.  B)   | 9.  C)  |
| 10. A)   | 11. C)  |
| 12. B)   | 13. B)  |
| 14. A)   | 15. A)  |
| 16. A)   | 17. C)  |
| 18. B)   | 19. C)  |
| 20. C)   |         |

21. The dashed white markings on the road indicate:
A) Passing is permitted
B) Vehicles traveling in the opposite direction
C) Passing is permissible as long as it is executed in a secure manner
D) Bicycles and motorcycles are specifically assigned to use the left lane.
22. Please determine the category of sign depicted in the image provided:
Cease

A) Surrender
B) drive with a leisurely pace
C) No Dangerous substances
23. When navigating a traffic circle, it is necessary to proceed:
A) In a counterclockwise manner.
B) Rotating in an anticlockwise manner.
C) Towards the approaching cars.
D) Towards any destination.
24. The designated sections on a two-lane road known as "turnout" areas serve the purpose of: A) Facilitating safe lane changes.
B) Move to change direction towards the opposite side.
C) Permit the passage of automobiles.
D) Permit drivers to come to a halt and utilize their mobile devices.

Answer Key:
    21.C)
    22.D)
    23.B)
    24.A)

## Test Quizz 6

1. What is the optimal course of action if sleepiness ensues while driving a car?

a) Speed up to enhance the gap between other vehicles.

b) Shift to the adjacent lane on the right and proceed with driving.

c) Proceed to a secure area, halt, and relax.

2. What actions should you take if the traffic signal is red but a law enforcement officer or firefighter on duty directs you to move forward?

a) Await the signal to proceed.

b) Abide by their directives.

c) Notify the authorities about them.

3. Within what timeframe are you required to notify the DMV of the sale or transfer of your vehicle?

a) 5 days

b) 10 days

c) 20 days

4. In what situation is it permissible to possess an unsealed alcoholic drink container in your automobile?

a) In the rear seat

b) Inside the boot

c) Within the glove box

5. What repercussions could you encounter if you amass several convictions for traffic infractions?

a) The Department of Motor Vehicles can seize your vehicle.

b) The Department of Motor Vehicles may revoke your vehicle operation ability.

c) Either of the options mentioned above.

When is "parallel parking" prohibited?

a) At any given moment

b) Except when making a shipment

c) Except when remaining inside the automobile

7. What are the obligations of cyclists when there is an absence of a designated lane for bicycles?

a) Travel in the direction of oncoming vehicles

b) Receive ample room when being overtaken by motorists

c) Avoid crossing the street on foot with the bicycle

8. Operating a vehicle at an excessively reduced speed to obstruct the regular movement of vehicles, unless required for safety purposes, is:

a) An infraction of the law

b) The privilege of any motorist

c) Lawful but not recommended

9. If a law enforcement officer requests you to submit to an alcohol examination, what alternatives are available?

a) A test that involves analyzing blood, breath, or urine samples

b) An assessment of motor skills and coordination

c) Repeat the alphabet in reverse order

10. What measures should you adopt if you are engaged in a collision?

a) Inform the nearby police department or California Highway Patrol (CHP) in case of any casualties or fatalities.

b) Display proof of insurance solely to a law enforcement officer.

c) Cease and ascertain your identity solely if someone is harmed.

11. What impact can sleep aids, sedatives, analgesics, or cold/allergy remedies have on your ability to operate a vehicle?

a) They could hinder your ability to drive.

b) They can worsen the adverse impacts of alcohol on your ability to operate a vehicle.

c) Both of the options mentioned above.

12. What might a passenger car be unable to haul?

a) A single mobile home

b) Yet another car

c) A pair of mobile homes

If a motorist in front of you has halted at a pedestrian crossing, what should be your course of action?

a) Switch lanes, observe, and overtake.

b) Honk your horn to inform the driver you are patiently waiting.

c) Halt, then continue when secure.

14. In what circumstances should you abstain from operating a vehicle?

a) Once you have ingested any beverage, substance, or remedy that hampers your mental faculties or behaviors

b) If you are not attentive.

c) Both of the options mentioned above.

15. When combining onto a motorway from an entrance ramp, at what velocity should you be driving to blend with traffic?

a) The lawful velocity restriction on the motorway.

b) Roughly equivalent velocity as the highway traffic.

c) Approximately 10 miles per hour less than the maximum speed allowed on the highway.

16. What is the condition of gliding with the gear shift in neutral?

a) Suggested in the hills.

b) Secure and preserves fuel.

c) Unlawful.

17. You are traveling beside a bike path and want to turn right at an intersection. What actions should you take?

a) run with the bicycle lane before making a turn.

b) Take your turn, ensuring to avoid the bicycle lane.

c) Indicate, search for cyclists, and continue with the maneuver.

18. When can you unlock your automobile's door on the side facing the flow of vehicles?

a) At any moment while stationary.

b) To depart but not to access your vehicle.

c) Solely when it is secure.

Where should you position your automobile if you are the initial individual to halt and offer aid at a crash site?

a) Once you have cleared the accident site. b) Before arriving at the crash scene.

c) Next to the accident site.

20. Following the 'implicit agreement law,' in what situations have you consented to undergo a blood alcohol test?

a) Every time you operate a vehicle in California.

b) Following the counsel of a lawyer.

c) If a mishap has taken place.

## Answer Key:

| 1. c) |
|---|
| 2. b) |
| 3. a) |
| 4. b) |
| 5. c) |
| 6. a) |
| 7. b) |
| 8. a) |
| 9. a) |
| 10. a) |
| 11. c) |
| 12. c) |
| 13. c) |
| 14. c) |
| 15. c) |
| 16. c) |
| 17. b) |
| 18. c) |
| 19. b) |
| 20. a) |

## Test quizz 7

1. You're moving slowly on the winding two-lane road. If you have any of the following, pull over as soon as it is safe to do so and allow oncoming traffic to pass:

   A. Three vehicles follow you

   B. four follow you

   C. five cars follow you.

   2. You should proceed cautiously without a STOP or YIELD sign at an "unseen" crossing (one where visibility is less than 100 feet). Limits of either

A) 15 miles per hour

B) 20 miles per hour

C) 25 miles per hour

3. U-turn can be performed in any lane when two lanes are available for a left turn at a junction.

b) Stick to the left side of the road.

c) The nearest open lane.

4. The right-of-way must be

a) always provided to pedestrians using guide dogs or white canes.

b) Only at junctions do drivers have the right of way.

c) Indicated the best moment to cross the street.

5. Always double-check for motorcycles when making a left turn or switching lanes since

a) they have the right-of-way.

b) Disappear in the background.

c) Travelling at high rates of speed.

6. If you hear a siren or see a police car, fire truck, or ambulance approaching, you must:
a) Pull over to the right shoulder of the road and stop.

b) Move to the right side of the road and go slowly until it passes.

b) Increase your speed and move quickly to avoid an accident.

7. Make sure it's safe to change lanes by performing the following before you do so:

a) swiveling your head to have a peek.

b) Check out the left-hand mirror.

c) Look at yourself in the rearview mirror.

8. To overtake another vehicle, you can go over the double queue if it is broken on your side of the road. Three solid colors are

a) red,

b) white

c) yellow.

9. whenever your temper rises to irritability or anger.Try

a) going for a drive to clear your

b) You should "cool off" before getting behind the wheel.

c) Keep yourself cool when you're driving.

10. Using a crosswalk or crossing the street

a) when the light is yellow or flashing red is against the law.

b) Because you'd be impeding traffic on both sides

c) crossing is risky.

11. How much do the following factors contribute to risky driving?

a) Make sure your parking lights are on at all times.

b) Focus on the vehicle in front of you at all times.

c) Check your intended direction of steering before making a turn.

12. It is perfectly lawful to do the following when a doctor prescribes a drug that might have an impact on driving: If the drug is for weight reduction or a cold, you can

a) drive

b) lawfully

c) legally.

d) all of the above

13. If you're driving on an interstate and see orange construction signs and cones, you should: a) slow down since the road is blocked.

a) be cautious.

b) Plan for slow workers and equipment.

c) Change lanes rapidly without braking.

14. If the cost of repairs for one of your vehicles is more than $750, state law mandates that you file a financial responsibility report.

15. When two cars are approaching a crossroads simultaneously

a) There are stop signs at all four (or more) corners

b) The driver on the right has the right of way.

c) It's a signal for making a turn.

16 Carpool lanes are indicated with a diamond symbol. To use these lanes during their designated hours, you must

a) drive a big passenger vehicle (such as a bus or van).

b) Always use your lights, and drive the speed limit.

c) Accommodate the specified number of passengers.

17. You will lose your driving privileges if you refuse a chemical test to detect your blood alcohol concentration after being pulled over on suspicion of drunk driving.

c) An additional fine will be assessed.

You can't have bail posted for you

18. If a flashing amber light is present at an intersection and you are preparing to traverse, you are required to:

a) Cease movement, When approaching a corner with a flashing yellow light, you must stop

b) Wait for the light to turn green before proceeding.

c) Cross the street slowly and carefully.

19. While operating a vehicle near a school where children are present, it is prohibited to exceed a speed limit of:

a) 35 miles per hour

b) 20 miles per hour

When passing a school where children are present, the speed limit is

a) 35 m.p.h.

b) 20 m.p.h.

c) 25 m.p.h.

20. There is empirical proof that seat belts:

a) could restrict drivers within their vehicles.

Twenty, some data suggest that wearing a seatbelt:

a) keeps drivers from moving about within their cars

b) makes it harder to maneuver in an emergency.

c) There's a chance that injury and death rates might go down.

21. If you and another automobile approach an intersection without any traffic signals or signs, it is necessary for you to yield to the subsequent drivers in the following sequence:

a) the driver positioned to your right

b) You must yield to the drivers on your right and left if you and another vehicle approach a junction without traffic lights or signs, respectively.

c) Nobody is at the wheel

22. You can assume that a moving vehicle whose right and left turn signals are flashing simultaneously is taking or dropping off students at a school.

a) At this intersection

b) you must give way to a vehicle.

c) A horrible event could occur shortly.

23. In California, drivers must consider the following: To comply with the "basic speed law" in California, drivers must consider both the maximum speed limit and any written speed restrictions.

a) lights timed to work together

, b) The weather, the amount of traffic

c) the condition of the road.

24. Once you arrive at a pedestrian crossing after traversing the roadway and observe a halt indication, after crossing the street, if you observe a stop sign in the crosswalk, you must) stop completely.

b) At a safe distance to see approaching traffic.

b) Past the path for pedestrians.

25. You are required to:

25. When nearing a stopped school bus with flashing red lights, reduce your speed to 10 mph. Until the flashing ceases,

a) Stop completely until the flashing

b) stops.

c) Change lanes and pass cautiously at a low speed.

Answer key:

| 1. c)  | 2. c)  |
|--------|--------|
| 3. c)  | 4. c)  |
| 5. a)  | 6. a)  |
| 7. b)  | 8. b)  |
| 9. b)  | 10. b) |
| 11. a) | 12. a) |
| 13. a) | 14. a) |
| 15. a) | 16. a) |

# Chapter 4: Safe and Conscious Driving

## Defensive driving and behavior on the road

Driving safety advice is among the most important reading a person can do, and it is essential to understand it when you are a novice driver.

Driving in California along a road next to the ocean may be a delight. It's especially annoying if you're caught in some of the world's worst traffic jams, such as in San Diego or Los Angeles. Anywhere you drive in this big state, you should constantly pay attention to the rules and regulations for driving.

Given that California has some of the largest motorways in the nation, many car accidents with corresponding injuries occur almost daily. If you drive one of those vehicles on a state highway, you should take safety measures to lower your risk of a collision. Here are some considerations for your lengthy drives.

### It is essential to have a laser-like concentration.

Focused drivers reduce the risk of auto accidents. These motorists are alert, perceptive, and unaffected by outside influences. All motorists in California must obey traffic laws and drive safely at all times. Follow these recommendations to drive defensively and maintain the safety of the roadways. Always be watchful, aware, and conscious.

You need to ensure they are awake and aware before driving. Make sure you can keep yourself attentive by sipping coffee or listening to music if you need to go urgently someplace but feel tired. Make wise decisions since music may sometimes be distracting as well. You need to be aware of your surroundings to drive responsibly. Drivers need to use caution and focus their attention on the road in front of them.

### Never drive when distracted.

Distracted driving is any action or behavior that takes your attention away from driving. According to the Centers for Disease Control (CDC), going while distracted may be either visual, tactile, or mental:

1. A visual activity takes your focus away from the road.

2. A tactile or manual distraction is any activity that requires you to take your hands off the wheel.

3. Cerebral or cognitive distractions include everything that takes your focus away from driving, including emotions, intrusive ideas, etc.

Several actions may be categorized as distracting in various ways. Your life and the lives of other drivers are at risk when you text and drive. Due to the many visual, physical, and mental distractions, it is quite dangerous. Here are some further instances of careless driving:

When you're talking on the phone or with your passengers, manually using your GPS, eating while driving, adjusting the radio's volume, or using social media apps.

### Daydreaming
Failure to pay attention to the road. Deadly threats might materialize in a matter of seconds.

### Before Operating a Motor Vehicle

- Are you alert, well-rested, and confident in your abilities to get where you're going?
- Make a vacation plan. Ask yourself whether you can do your assignment without a car at all. Is a phone call, email, or online meeting a viable way to reduce wasted driving? Are there any hazards associated with using public transportation?
- Using transportation services and shared taxis are two options for reducing driving time.
- If you must drive, make a schedule in advance. Even if it's only a little vacation, some helpful web resources are available to aid with your planning.
- Make a travel schedule - Examine the routes you anticipate taking and plan a backup path if anything goes wrong. Observe the flow of traffic, the severity of the weather, and the state of the roads. Even poor weather may sometimes cause problems. If you are prone to sun blindness when driving, make sure you have a pair of sunglasses on you at all times. Establish a check-in proof and let your manager know what you have planned.
- Make your automobile comfortable by adjusting the headrest, seat, and rearview mirrors as needed. Make a pre-trip inspection to make sure everything is in working condition. Exists any upkeep that must be completed? Talk to your technician if you don't believe the automobile is capable. Take damaged vehicles for short trips only.
- Since other drivers may not be paying attention to the road, you must remain vigilant on their behalf. It's essential to be a cautious driver who can evaluate possible dangers and traffic situations. By actively watching and focusing on the road, drivers may help reduce auto accidents.

# Dealing with adverse weather conditions
When the seasons change, everyone loses their driving skills. It's an unavoidable reality.

Driving too fast and following too closely is the leading cause of fatal crashes in California and is the main contributor to winter and early spring collisions. We sometimes overlook that stopping distances are larger on icy, snowy, or slushy roadways.

For a review of safe driving practices under bad road and weather conditions, follow the following advice or give it to a buddy who forgets things.

## Rule #1: Check Your Speed first.

The greatest speed you can drive under the ideal road and weather conditions is indicated by speed limits on roads and highways. When going in less-than-ideal circumstances (such as on wet, slick, slushy, or snow-covered roads or in the rain, snow, or fog), you should:

- Modify your speed and go more slowly.
- Maintain a speed that will allow you to drive your car safely.
- Avoid using cruise control on slick or wet roads.
- If you can see less than 15 to 20 seconds in front of you, slow down.
·Approach highway repair vehicles carefully, and never pass on the right.

## Rule #2: Leave Some Room

Compared to driving on dry pavement, stopping your car on soft or loose snow may take up to three times as long, and preventing it on icy winter roads can take up to 12 times as long. Keeping a minimum of 3 seconds between you and the car you are following can help you gauge how much distance to allow between your vehicle and the one in front of you.

- Pay attention to the car in front of you.
- Start counting (one-thousand-and-one, one-thousand-and-two, one-thousand-and-three) when the rear of that vehicle passes a fixed object, such as a sign, tree, or road marker.
- You are following too closely if the front of your car approaches the item before you have completed counting.
- Recount as you reduce the speed of your car. You must re-adjust your three-second following distance if someone cuts before you.
- When driving on terrain with little traction, the three-second rule has to be increased. Drivers of big commercial vehicles are the only ones who should utilize a minimum 4-second following distance in traffic.

## Rule #3: Never Stop in Traffic

Always try to find a way to get out of the way while stopped in traffic.
- Give the car stopped at least one vehicle space in front of you. If the road surface turns out to be more slick than you thought, this will prevent you from slamming into it. Any time you brake or accelerate, such as at an intersection or in a curve, the road is slippery during the winter.
- Give yourself some room in case you are stopped behind a stalled car in traffic or are hit from behind by another vehicle.
- Always proceed with care while stopping behind a big car going uphill.

## Rule #4: Before Departing

- Be ready and dressed appropriately, even if traveling a few blocks.
- Clean your windows, lights, and windshield to improve your visibility.
- Maintain a full tank of gas. In addition to lowering the chance that you'll run out of petrol while traveling, a less-than-full tank is more susceptible to condensation and may result in gas lines freezing.

# How to avoid distractions behind the wheel

Any action that diverts your attention from driving, such as talking on the phone or texting, eating or drinking, engaging in conversation with passengers, or utilizing the navigation or entertainment system, is considered distracted driving. The most popular kind of distraction is texting. Did you realize that sending or reading a simple text requires five seconds or more of your attention away from the road? This is equivalent to driving a football field with your eyes closed at 55 mph.

The plain truth is that you can only drive safely if you give the road in front of you all your attention. Applying cosmetics, eating a bagel, or sipping coffee for breakfast are all non-driving activities that increase your chance of colliding with anything.

The following list of 19 strategies can help you stay focused while driving.

### #1: Put your phone in an airplane or do not disturb mode while driving.

Put your phone in the glove box or the back seat until you reach your destination if you can't resist touching it.

### #2: Regularly clean your windshield.

Make sure your wiper fluid is sufficient. Any obstruction might slow down your response time.

### #3: Avoid using cosmetics while driving.

This distracts you from the road and might be deadly if you collide. That mascara wand might pierce your eye!

### #4: Abstain from food and liquids.

Adding milk to your coffee or grabbing the takeout bag's fries may seem innocent, but doing so diverts your attention from the road for a little period.

## #5: Minimize passenger distractions.

Save long debates or disputes for another time. Your focus is on something other than the road when it is on what you'll say next.

## #6: Let go of fallen objects.

Let it go if you drop your phone, your bag falls over, or your kid leaves a toy in the backseat. If you need to get it, stop.

## #7: Immediately remove any rolling balls.

Pullover carefully if you see a ball that has gotten free and is rolling about. Your brake and gas pedals may get jammed with hops, which may cause a tragic accident. Better, better, don't let balls into the vehicle in the first place.

## #8: Avoid texting at stop signs.

The majority of individuals are aware that it is not appropriate to text while driving, yet they nonetheless take out their phones at red lights. Red lights still need your attention to see when it turns green, and watch out for other drivers who could be inattentive.

## #9. Avoid becoming sidetracked by the children and pets in the backseat.

Youngsters who are crying, delighted youngsters, and excitable canines may all vie for your attention. Please focus on the road ahead and tune them out.

## #10: Refrain from turning up the volume.

Everyone enjoys cranking up their favorite music on a warm summer day. However, strong sounds can make it difficult to hear important environmental cues like approaching police cars or ambulances.

## #11.Avoid rubbernecking (rule 11).

Even though we all do it, we still resent the idiots who block traffic to inspect an accident on the side of the road. Move on and concentrate on your security.

## #12: Refrain from staring at parked cars.

Express your gratitude that it's not you and pass the policeman stopping another motorist.

## #13 Avoid tailgating

The California DMV advises adhering to the "3-second rule": when the car in front of you crosses a certain point, such as a landmark or sign, count "one-thousand-one, one-thousand-two, one-thousand-three." It takes three seconds to do this. You are following the automobile in front of you too closely if you pass that location before you have completed counting.

## #14 Avoid unruly travelers

Give your adolescent driver some sound advice. Tell them to turn off the radio, tell their pals to unwind, and reserve the enjoyment for when they arrive. Significant causes of distraction include friends who shout, bounce around, and create a commotion.

## #15: Use your visor and wear sunglasses.

Make sure to have your sunglasses on hand and your visor down during periods of maximum solar glare, such as dawn and sunset.

## #16: Never drive while smoking.

Smoking a cigarette while operating a vehicle might temporarily divert your attention, causing you to miss an important cue.

## #17: Avoid doing simple grooming duties.

Avoid shaving, adjusting your clothing, and doing your hair while driving, much like applying cosmetics.

## #18: Never raise your convertible top in a busy area.

You can do this in certain vehicles with the click of a button. This does not imply that you need to do it while driving. To safely put the top on, pull over.

## #19: Avoid overreacting to external stimuli.

Keep your eyes straight ahead and ignore it if someone honks or screams at you in rage. These are pointless diversionary activities that may divert your focus from the road. By refusing to participate in this activity, you also resist the need to act out in anger on the road, which might lead to a terrible disaster.

Most of us have engaged in one or more of these behaviors. We must commit to change, work to improve, and be more aware of our surroundings.

# Chapter 5: California-Specific Driving Regulations

## Speed limits and parking rules

### Limits on speed

Pace restrictions are implemented to provide drivers with a clear directive to go at a pace that, under normal circumstances, enables a safe and orderly traffic flow.

"Basic Speed Law" in California states that "No person shall drive a vehicle upon a highway at a speed greater than is reasonable or prudent having due regard for the weather, visibility, the traffic on, and the surface and width of, the highway, and in no event at a speed which endangers the safety of persons or property." The majority of California's roadways have a 65 mph maximum speed restriction. The top speed restriction is 55 mph on two-lane undivided roads and for cars carrying trailers unless otherwise marked.

The following statutory speed restrictions are also established by the California Vehicle Code (CVC):

• In alleyways, at blind crossroads, and railroad crossings with blind spots, 15 mph.

• 25 mph in residential and commercial areas, school zones, kid-friendly playgrounds, and senior citizen facilities.

**These speed restrictions may or may not be displayed.**

Speed zoning is setting fair and safe speed restrictions for certain stretches of road. Engineering and traffic surveys are used to determine non-statutory speed restrictions. This survey produces an acceptable speed restriction by considering variables including the kind of nearby development, pedestrian and bicycle activity, roadside conditions, reported crash history, and the current traffic speed. The prevalent speed is the pace at which 85% of drivers are moving. Based on the assumption that most drivers adhere to an acceptable speed restriction, the overall speed is used as a benchmark for setting speed limits. According to studies, adopting arbitrary low-speed limits leads to widespread infractions rather than necessarily lowering driving speeds.

### California Parking Regulations

In California, parking restrictions are indicated by the color of the curb.

The meanings of each color are as follows:

- **White**-only passenger pick-up and drop-off stops are permitted for moving vehicles. Drivers should typically stay inside the car.

Parking is permitted on the green side. A time restriction, nevertheless, is indicated by signage or painted on the curb.

- **Yellow** - Passenger and freight loading and unloading are permitted but should not exceed the stipulated time restriction. Drivers should remain inside their non-commercial vehicle while using it.

- **Red** - it's not permitted to park, halt, or stand. Buses may stop on a red curb if a zone designated for buses is present.

- **Blue** - Parking spaces reserved for people with disabilities or those driving them. Only vehicles with license plates or placards for disabled veterans or people can park here.

In addition, notwithstanding the time restrictions indicated on the signage, those with disabilities who have a placard can utilize the parking space for any period.

Loss of parking rights and up to 6 months in jail or a $1000 fine result from using a disabled person's license plate improperly.

## California illegal parking

What if the curb you wish to park on doesn't have a color code?

It's crucial to know where parking in California is prohibited now.

So, the following locations are prohibited for parking:

When a "No Parking" sign is in front of a driveway, on the sidewalk, when you're partly blocking a side street, at a designated or unmarked crossing, or next to a ramp for people with disabilities.

- Within 15 feet of a fire hydrant or station driveway

Double parking

When all available parking places are used.

- In a parking space for disabled people if you don't have a disabled license • In the diagonal lines or the crosshatched area next to the accessible parking space • In a parking space for refueling zero-emission vehicles if you don't own one • Between the curb and a safety zone • On the wrong side of the road, except emergencies, when it is permitted to stop, or when a law enforcement officer requests it.

## California's parking laws carry penalties.

What happens if you violate these parking regulations in California?
You will be subject to fines and citations for certain offenses.
The following table lists the parking infraction and fines:

| One Way Traffic | Penalty |
| --- | --- |
| One Way Traffic | $50 |
| One Way Traffic | $50 |
| One Way Traffic | $100 |
| One Way Traffic | $50 |
| One Way Traffic | $35 |
| One Way Traffic | $50 |
| One Way Traffic | $35 |
| One Way Traffic | $35 |
| One Way Traffic | $35 |

| | |
|---|---|
| One Way Traffic | $445 |
| One Way Traffic | $35 |
| One Way Traffic | $23 |
| One Way Traffic | $35 |
| One Way Traffic | $35 |
| One Way Traffic | $445 |
| One Way Traffic | $445 |
| One Way Traffic | $100 |
| One Way Traffic | $50 |
| One Way Traffic | $52 |
| One Way Traffic | $57 |
| One Way Traffic | $53 |

You can be required to pay extra if

- Any statutory fees must be applied to the penalties for parking infractions.

- If a cost of collection arises, the cost shall be increased, and the offender shall be accountable; • If no request or payment has been made within the period specified by law, an extra delinquency penalty shall be imposed

## Tips for safe parking

Okay, now that you know the California parking regulations and the associated fines, let's move on to practical advice for safe parking.

### 1. Parking on side

The following cautions apply while parking parallel to the road:

1. Look for a parking spot at least 3 feet longer than your car.

2. remember to switch on your signal when performing the move.

3. Approach the car in front of the parking place of your choice. Keep spacing approximately 2 feet between your vehicle and the one next to it. Once your parking place is in front of the back bumper, stop.

4. After checking your rearview mirror, put your car in reverse.

5. Rotate your wheels at a 45-degree angle to back into the parking place.

6. Straighten your parking by pushing forward or backward while rotating the steering wheel away from the curb. Your car will now parallel the curb and be around 18 inches away.

## 2. Parking on a Hill

It's more complex than you may assume to find parking on a hill. Your car could slide down if your brakes fail. Here are some suggestions to prevent this:

- To avoid rolling your car into the street if the brakes fail, spin the wheels while parking on a sloped driveway.

- When traveling downhill, position the parking brake and move the front wheels toward the curb or the side of the road.

- Turn the front wheels away from the curb while traveling uphill. When you are a few inches from the curb, carefully let the reels contact it. Parking brake set.

- If there isn't a curb and you're going up or downhill, and there isn't one, turn your wheels toward the road to prevent the car from veering off the middle if your brakes fail.

# Rules for drivers of commercial vehicles

Usually, commercial vehicles and their drivers must abide by specific state and federal rules. Due to their size, commercial trucks may severely damage smaller automobiles in collisions. Such a danger is intended to be reduced by the specific rules for such vehicles. The definition of a commercial vehicle under California law and additional regulations that apply to such vehicles are shown below.

## Commercial vehicles: what are they?

According to California law, a commercial vehicle is any vehicle used to convey people or goods. A car is considered in this category when it is used to carry people for employment, payment, or profit.

Some of the cars that must be registered as commercial vehicles by these requirements are those listed below:

- Vehicles with several uses

- Passenger-type automobiles

- Larger vehicles; station wagons; and pickup trucks

## California Commercial Vehicle and Driver Laws

Every commercial driver operating in California is required to adhere to several state and federal rules. These laws often cover the following areas:

Regulations for hours of operation, speed restrictions, lane regulations, and cargo restrictions

## Rules for Hours of Service

The exhaustion of the driver of a commercial vehicle is one of the main factors in many collisions. To earn more money, drivers often drive for longer periods, or their employers may need it for business reasons. However, it is against the law for a driver to operate any commercial vehicle when they are either unwell or exhausted.

The rule mandates that commercial drivers pull over if they experience any impairment, including sickness symptoms, weariness, or sleepiness. To further clarify this, the FMCA establishes hours of service requirements that cap the total number of hours a driver may operate a vehicle without a break. Depending on their schedule and whether the truck is transporting people or freight, a commercial driver may drive for a certain amount of hours in a shift.

## Property-Carrying Vehicles and Their Drivers
Commercial vehicle drivers can only operate for 11 hours after taking 10 off. They are only allowed to drive for 14 hours in a row after a 10-hour rest.

## Drivers of Passenger-Carrying Vehicles
Drivers who transport passengers may work a maximum of 10 hours in a row without interruption. Similarly, they can only drive for up to 15 hours following an 8-hour rest. Both types of drivers are prohibited from operating a truck for more than 60 straight hours in a row over seven days or more than 70 hours over eight days.

## Rules for Pull-Over or Sleeper Berths

Additionally, the FMCSA sets rules that call for truck drivers to stop if they get fatigued and rest in their sleeper berths after extended periods of driving. A driver may get weary and cause accidents if he violates the hours of service regulations. Similarly, a business may be held responsible for accidents or losses if it encourages drivers to break the hours of service law in exchange for bonuses or other incentives.

## California's new law on unpaid time off

California has enacted brand-new legislation. Due to this regulation, trucking businesses in California are no longer required to pay their drivers during break times. The driver cannot choose to forego the break, though. In California, all drivers must take breaks every four hours for ten minutes and every five hours for thirty minutes.

## Speed restrictions

Accidents often result from commercial trucks traveling at excessive speeds. The legislation establishes speed restrictions for commercial vehicles to reduce such occurrences. Commercial vehicles must adhere to rigorous regulations and may not travel at speeds more than 10 miles per hour in certain locations. Some commercial vehicles must drive at a maximum speed of 55 mph on highways. These include

- Tractors and trucks with three or more axles
- Tractors and trucks towing another vehicle.
- Vehicles carrying explosives, farm laborers transporting people, school buses carrying pupils, and the Lane Rule

You must remain in the right-hand lane of the road or a lane specifically marked for slow-moving vehicles if you are driving a truck, bus, or car with a second component in towing. Only the two right-hand lanes may be used while driving on a road with four or more lanes.

## Cargo Laws

In California, the following must be done by businesses and drivers:

- Make sure the goods are spread evenly and securely on the vehicle
- Tie or load the cargo appropriately
- Thoroughly inspect the cargo or property

# What to do in case of traffic accidents

What actions should you take right away after a vehicle accident? While property damage is the most common effect of automobile accidents, the driver or passengers are injured in around 30% of collisions. Here is a list of immediate actions you should do if you were hurt in an accident to safeguard your rights and well-being:

## STOP AND STAY AT THE SCENE

You must wait for the police to arrive at the accident site. Never drive away after a collision without exchanging contact details with the other motorist. In the future, leaving the scene too quickly might hurt your legal rights.

## DEFEND YOURSELF

•Before exiting the car, be sure it is secure to do so. Your hazard lights should be on. If the collision happens in the middle of the motorway or another unsafe location, stay inside your car and lock all the doors.

## CALL 911 FOR THE POLICE

Having the police or the California Highway Patrol records the collision can be helpful when completing your insurance claim. Be careful to ask the officers for the police report number and get a copy of your police record as soon as possible. Whenever the offer of an ambulance is made, accept it.

## SUBMISSION OF A POLICE REPORT

When there aren't any major injuries or evidence of alcohol or drug use, the police may sometimes decline to file a report. However, keep in mind that even if you don't immediately experience any pain, it's likely that your adrenaline surge is keeping you from seeing the damage. You should request that the police write a report, record all witnesses' comments, and note everyone's contact information. Make sure everything is correct when you get a copy of this report.

## PRESERVE VISUAL EVIDENCE

If you don't agree with any part of the report, go to the police station and ask to have it changed to reflect the accurate facts. Please take photographs of each involved vehicle, the damage it has sustained, and any debris or road markings. In your scenario, the existence or lack of skid marks on the road may be crucial. If you were harmed, document the damage as soon as possible. You should also maintain taking photos of your wounds as your recovery advances.

## COLLECT AND EXCHANGE CONTACT AND INSURANCE DATA

If the police were called to the incident, the officers would compile the necessary data and include it in the police report. The names, addresses, and phone numbers of everyone present, including the other drivers, witnesses, and bystanders, should be recorded if the police do not respond.

## GET MEDICAL CARE RIGHT AWAY

Do not assume you were not hurt even if you do not immediately experience unpleasant symptoms. Most soft tissue and whiplash injuries appear hours or even days after the trauma. Following the accident, you should seek emergency medical assistance if you feel pain or discomfort in any area of your body.

Serious spinal injuries are possible, especially in rear-end accident instances. Left untreated and undiagnosed, these injuries may leave a person permanently disabled and handicapped. You should have a neurological follow-up if you struck your head, fainted, or briefly lost consciousness to treat brain damage or post-concussive symptoms.

Following the event, if you have any changes in your mood or memory, it might be an indication of severe brain damage.

### Assess your development and pinpoint areas that want improvement.

I can give you some broad pointers on how to assess your development and pinpoint your weak points in preparation for the DMV California exam:

Use practice exams to check your knowledge and pinpoint areas where you need help. DMV practice exams for California are available online from various sites, and they may help you become used to the style and kinds of questions you could see on the real test.

**Review Your Results:** After completing practice exams, examine your results to see which questions you properly answered and which you didn't. Pay close attention to the places where you erred or were uncertain.

**Study Your Weak Areas:** Pay particular attention to the subjects or regions of the practice exam you performed poorly in. To improve your understanding, spend more time studying the relevant areas of the DMV manual.

**Use Study Materials:** Consult the California DMV's official handbooks, manuals, and study materials. These sites will cover all the material you need to know for the test.

Review the traffic regulations, road signs, and driving legislation in California. To guarantee you can recognize them throughout the test, familiarize yourself with frequent traffic signs and their explanations.

**Simulate exam settings:** When confident in the material, try completing a full-length practice exam in a timed environment to mimic test settings. This will enable you to acclimate to the test's pressure and time limits.

**Seek explanation:** Be bold and ask for answers from reliable sources, such as driving instructors or online discussion groups for driving examinations, if you encounter any confusing ideas or problems.

## Be Confident and Serenity:
1. On the test day, strive to maintain your confidence and peace.
2. Stay away from last-minute studying and have faith in your preparedness.
3. During the exam, be concentrated and thoroughly read each question before responding.

Remember that the DMV test in California is intended to promote responsible driving and road safety. Spend some time studying and getting ready. If you don't succeed on your first try, analyze the situation to see what needs to change, then learn more before attempting again. I wish you luck on your test!

• Get ready for test day • Being well-prepared for the California DMV exam will help you pass with flying colors. Here are some helpful hints to aid in your preparation:

Study the Driver's Handbook: Read the DMV-provided California Driver Handbook. It covers all the fundamental laws, regulations of the road, and road signs you need to be aware of for the test.

**Take practice tests:** They are quite helpful for helping you get comfortable with the structure of the actual exam and for allowing you to pinpoint areas you need to improve. You may utilize authentic exams from the California DMV website or free online practice tests.

Please pay attention to the traffic signs and comprehend their respective meanings. As there will be numerous questions on traffic signs on the test, memorize their colors and forms.

Understand the many traffic laws governing right-of-way, speed limits, parking regulations, etc. Understanding these laws can help you accurately respond to questions on the test.

**Practice Safe Driving:** While you're studying, put safety first while you're driving. Learn the proper driving techniques and safety precautions.

**Time Management:**
1. Use your time carefully on the day of the test.
2. Take your time on any one question.
3. Move on and return to the question later if you need more confidence about the answer.

**Receive Lots of Sleep:** The night before the test, ensure you get a good night's sleep. You will perform better and maintain concentration if you get enough sleep.

**Arrive Early:** On exam day, arrive at the testing facility early. You'll have plenty of time to unwind and check your notes before the exam.

**Bring the Required Documents:** Remember to bring any documentation the DMV may need, identification, and proof of residence.

Remember to be composed and confident during the test. You can correctly respond to the questions confidently in your knowledge and preparedness.

You'll have a better chance of passing the California DMV test if you adhere to this advice and remain dedicated to your study plan. Good fortune!

# Chapter 6: Comprehensive Practice Tests
# Complete DMV exam simulations

## Quizz 1

1. When you see an emergency vehicle with its lights flashing on the wrong side of the road, giving instructions through the loudspeaker, you should:

a) Immediately pull over to the side of the road and stop.

b) Continue driving at the same speed, ignoring the emergency vehicle.

c) Follow the instructions given by the emergency vehicle.

d) Honk your horn to signal the emergency vehicle to move.

2. What does this road sign indicate?

[Image: A road sign with a picture of a deer]

a) Deer crossing area ahead.

b) No entry for deer.

c) Animal zoo nearby.

d) Slow down and watch for pedestrians.

3. What is the correct hand signal for indicating a right turn?

a) Extend your left arm horizontally out of the window.

b) Extend your right arm horizontally out of the window.

c) Extend your left arm and hand upward.

d) Extend your left arm and hand downward.

4. A _____ indicates the outer edge of a roadway, and it may be crossed only by traffic moving to or from the shoulder.

a) Solid white line.

b) Broken white line.

c) Solid yellow line.

d) Broken yellow line.

5. Vehicles approaching a roundabout must:

a) Come to a complete stop before entering the roundabout.

b) Yield to traffic already in the roundabout and pedestrians in the crosswalk.

c) Speed up to quickly merge into the roundabout.

d) Sound their horn to alert other drivers of their presence.

6. When turning right into a two-way street, start in the right-hand lane and enter into:

a) The left lane of the two-way street.

b) Any lane that is available.

c) The nearest lane to the right curb or edge of the roadway.

d) The center lane of the two-way street.

7. Which of the following right-of-way rules is FALSE?

a) Vehicles already in the intersection have the right-of-way.

b) Vehicles turning left must yield to oncoming traffic and pedestrians.

c) Vehicles entering a main road from a private driveway must yield to oncoming traffic.

d) Vehicles turning right must always yield to vehicles turning left.

8. The primary traveling aids for a blind person include:

a) Flashlights.

b) Guide dogs.

c) Walkie-talkies.

d) Bicycles.

9. On a two-way roadway with a center lane, drivers from either direction can _____ from the center lane.

a) Make U-turns.

b) Pass other vehicles.

c) Park their vehicles.

d) Turn left.

10. The octagonal shape in the figure is:

a) A yield sign.

b) A stop sign.

c) An advisory speed sign.

d) A pedestrian crossing sign

11. You are driving slowly on a two-lane road. If there are at least ____ vehicles behind you that are unable to pass you, you must pull over and allow them to pass.

a) Two.

b) Three.

c) Five.

d) Ten

12. Flag persons are often located on highways and in work zones:

a) To provide information about nearby tourist attractions.

b) To direct traffic through detours.

c) To enforce speeding laws.

d) To sell souvenirs to drivers.

13. What does this flashing arrow panel mean?

Image: A road sign with a flashing arrow pointing left]

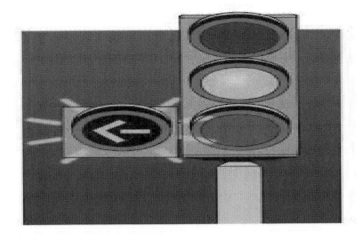

a) Construction work is completed; proceed at normal speed.
b) Merge left due to construction work ahead.
c) Warning of a sharp left turn in the road ahead.
d) Proceed with caution; traffic is being directed to the left lane.

14. With any turning vehicle, the rear wheels follow a _____ than the front wheels.

a) Shorter path.
b) Longer path.
c) Path of the same length.
d) Zigzag path.

15. Car drivers should NEVER:

a) Check blind spots before changing lanes.
b) Drive while under the influence of alcohol or drugs.
c) Signal when turning or changing lanes.
d) Yield to pedestrians in crosswalks.

16. This hand signal indicates that:

[Image: A hand extended out of a car window, palm facing backward]

a) The driver is slowing down or stopping.

b) The driver is making a left turn.

c) The driver is making a right turn.

d) The driver is angry at another driver.

17. This sign warns that:

[Image: A road sign with a wavy line indicating a slippery road]

a) There is a construction zone ahead.

b) The road is slippery when wet.

c) Drivers should slow down and watch for pedestrians.

d) The road ahead is closed.

18. If you see two solid yellow lines on a roadway, it means that:

a) Overtaking and passing other vehicles are allowed.

b) No passing is allowed in either direction.

c) Passing is allowed only during daylight hours.

d) Passing is allowed, but only for slow-moving vehicles.

19. On two-lane highways, you are allowed to pass:

a) On hills and curves.

b) Only on the left side of the road.

c) Only if the vehicle in front of you is going too slow.

d) Only if there is a passing lane marked on the road.

**Answers key:**

| 1. c)   | 2. a)  |
|---------|--------|
| 3. d)   | 4. a)  |
| 5. b)   | 6. c)  |
| 7. d)   | 8. b)  |
| 9. a)   | 10. b) |
| 11. b)  | 12. b) |
| 13. d)  | 14. b) |
| 15. d). | 16. a) |
| 17. b)  | 18. b) |
| 19. A)  |        |

# Quizz 2

1. If a pedestrian is in a marked or unmarked crosswalk, you must:

a) Slow down and proceed with caution.

b) Honk to alert the pedestrian.

c) Speed up to pass the pedestrian quickly.

d) Maintain your speed and continue driving.

2. An _____ is the connection of a freeway to a road or another freeway by a series of 2. ramps.

a) Overpass.

b) Underpass.

c) Interchange.

d) Intersection.

3. A two-headed arrow with one head pointing straight ahead and the other pointing to the left means that:

a) Only left turns are allowed at the intersection.

b) Only right turns are allowed at the intersection.

c) Both straight ahead and left turns are allowed at the intersection.

d) Drivers must proceed in the direction of the left-pointing arrow.

4. If you are parallel parked on the right-hand side of the street, you should _____ before pulling out into traffic.

a) Turn on your hazard lights.

b) Sound your horn to alert other drivers.

c) Yield to pedestrians and oncoming traffic.

d) Make a U-turn before pulling out.

5. A triangular orange sign on the rear of a vehicle indicates that:

a) The vehicle is carrying hazardous materials.

b) The vehicle is moving slowly.

c) The vehicle is making a wide turn.

d) The vehicle is a slow-moving construction vehicle.

6. At an intersection, a steady yellow arrow signal pointing left indicates to the driver that:

a) They must prepare to stop.

b) They may proceed cautiously in the left direction.

c) They must make a U-turn.

d) They must yield to oncoming traffic.

7. If temperatures are near freezing, which freezes first?

a) Wet roads.

b) Bridges and overpasses.

c) Grassy areas.

d) Sidewalks.

8. Which of the following statements about the right-of-way is FALSE?

a) The vehicle on the right has the right-of-way at an uncontrolled intersection.

b) Pedestrians always have the right-of-way at marked crosswalks.

c) Vehicles turning left must yield to oncoming traffic and pedestrians.

d) The vehicle entering a traffic circle or roundabout has the right-of-way over vehicles already in the circle.

9. Flashing yellow lights on a school bus require other drivers to:

a) Pass the bus carefully.

b) Stop until the lights stop flashing.

c) Slow down and proceed with caution.

d) Speed up to avoid congestion.

10. When approaching an intersection to make a right turn, you must stay _____ and make the turn close to the right curb.

a) In the center of the intersection.

b) In any lane that is available.

c) In the left lane.

d) In the right lane.

11. While driving, when you see a triangular road sign, you must:

a) Come to a complete stop.

b) Proceed with caution.

c) Make a U-turn.

d) Slow down to 20 mph.

12. You may pass a stopped light-rail vehicle on the left side:

a) If the rail has more than one track.

b) Only when passengers are not getting on or off the light-rail vehicle.

c) If the light-rail vehicle is in a designated lane for vehicles.

d) Never.

13. Which of the following are used as left-edge lines on divided highways?

a) White solid lines.

b) White broken lines.

c) Yellow solid lines.

d) Yellow broken lines.

14. If a driver extends his or her left arm out horizontally, it indicates that the driver is going to:

a) Turn right.

b) Turn left.

c) Come to a sudden stop.

d) Speed up.

15. On two-lane roads where traffic moves in opposite directions, you may pass on the left only when:

a) The driver in front of you is driving below the speed limit.

b) You are approaching a curve or hill.

c) You have a clear view of oncoming traffic and can safely pass.

d) The driver in front of you signals that it's safe to pass.

16. Do not use your horn:

a) In emergencies to avoid collisions.

b) To greet other drivers.

c) To alert pedestrians of your presence.

d) To indicate your annoyance or frustration.

17. one-way roads, yellow lines are used as:

a) Center lines.

b) Left-edge lines.

c) Right-edge lines.

d) No-passing lines.

18. If you approach an intersection with a steady yellow light, you must:

a) Proceed through the intersection without stopping.

b) Come to a complete stop and wait for the green light.

c) Slow down and prepare to stop.

d) Speed up to clear the intersection before the light turns red.

19. _____ occurs on wet roads when your front tires start to ride on water instead of on the road.

a) Skidding.

b) Hydroplaning.

c) Sliding.

d) Traction loss.

20. Which of the following statements about passing a vehicle is FALSE?

a) You should only pass when it is safe and legal to do so.

b) Always check your blind spots before attempting to pass.

c) It is acceptable to exceed the speed limit while passing.

d) Signal your intention to pass before changing lanes.

**Short Answers Key:**

1. Slow down and proceed with caution.
2. Interchange.
3. Both straight ahead and left turns are allowed at the intersection.
4. Yield to pedestrians and oncoming traffic.
5. The vehicle is carrying hazardous materials.
6. They may proceed cautiously in the left direction.
7. Bridges and overpasses.
8. Vehicles turning left must yield to oncoming traffic and pedestrians.
9. Stop until the lights stop flashing.
10. In the right lane.
11. Proceed with caution.
12. Never.
13. Yellow broken lines.
14. Turn left.
15. You have a clear view of oncoming traffic and can safely pass.
16. To greet other drivers.
17. Right-edge lines.
18. Slow down and prepare to stop.
19. Hydroplaning.
20. It is acceptable to exceed the speed limit while passing.

## Quizz 3

1. You may not cross a double solid yellow line on your left to:

a) Pass other vehicles.

b) Turn left into a driveway.

c) Make a U-turn.

d) Park your vehicle.

2. When you approach a roundabout, you must enter to the _____ of the central island.

a) Right.

b) Left.

c) Either side.

d) Farthest side.

3. What does this sign mean?

[Image: A sign with a picture of a bicycle]

a) Bicycle parking area ahead.

b) Bicycles not allowed.

c) Watch for bicycles.

d) Bicycles must yield.

4. When you turn off a high-speed, two-lane roadway, _____ if you have traffic following you.

a) Speed up.

b) Slow down.

c) Use your hazard lights.

d) Signal and pull onto the shoulder.

5. Your vehicle breaks down on a freeway. You are not able to move the vehicle off the road completely as the road shoulder is too narrow. What is the best thing to do?

a) Stay inside the vehicle and call for assistance.

b) Turn on your hazard lights and wait for help.

c) Try to fix the vehicle yourself.

d) Exit the vehicle and stand away from traffic.

6. Blind pedestrians may carry _____ canes or use guide dogs.

a) White and red.

b) Green and white.

c) Black and white.

d) Yellow and red.

7. When you park and leave your vehicle on a highway or street, you should NOT:

a) Leave the engine running.

b) Set the parking brake.

c) Turn off the ignition.

d) Leave the vehicle in neutral.

8. Which of these signs indicates a hospital ahead?

[Image: A sign with an "H" inside a blue square]

a) White text on a red octagon.

b) Black text on a yellow triangle.

c) A sign with an "H" inside a blue square

d) Black text on a white rectangle with a red circle and red border

9. All regulatory devices on the road tell you:

a) The distance to the nearest town.

b) The speed at which you must drive.

c) Information about nearby attractions.

d) The rules to follow.

10. It is unsafe for you to pass when:

a) You are on a one-way road.

b) The vehicle in front is going too slowly.

c) Approaching a railroad crossing.

d) Driving through an intersection.

11. _____ are the most likely places for car and motorcycle collisions to occur.

a) Roundabouts.

b) Tunnels.

c) Intersections.

d) Freeways.

12. What does this sign indicate?

[Image: A sign with a picture of a deer]

a) Deer crossing area ahead.

b) Animal zoo nearby.

c) Wildlife prohibited.

d) Hunting permitted.

13. 1If you are approaching a stop sign, you must:

a) Slow down and be prepared to stop if necessary.

b) Speed up to clear the intersection quickly.

c) Stop only if there is cross-traffic.

d) Honk your horn to alert other drivers.

14. What is the first rule of a safe and legal turn?

a) Always come to a complete stop before turning.

b) Use your turn signal to indicate your intention to turn.

c) Turn into the lane closest to the centerline.

d) Yield to oncoming traffic and pedestrians.

15. A yield sign indicates that a driver must slow down and be prepared to _____ if a vehicle or pedestrian with the right-of-way is approaching from another direction.

a) Come to a complete stop.

b) Change lanes.

c) Merge.

d) Yield the right-of-way.

16. Before backing up your vehicle, you should look to the front, sides, and rear, and continue to look _____ while backing.

a) Only to the rear.

b) Only to the front.

c) Only to the sides.

d) In all directions.

17. In California, the speed limit for a blind intersection is:

a) 25 mph.

b) 35 mph.

c) 15 mph.

d) 45 mph.

18. You must use your high-beam headlights in all of the following situations, except:

a) Driving in heavy fog.

b) Driving on an unlit country road.

c) Approaching a vehicle from behind at night.

d) Driving in a well-lit urban area.

19. Before reaching the crest of a hill or entering a curve, you must _____, and watch for oncoming vehicles.

a) Turn on your hazard lights.

b) Slow down and be prepared to stop.

c) Flash your high-beam headlights.

d) Speed up to get over the hill quickly.

20. If a tire suddenly goes flat while you're driving, you should:

a) Brake immediately to stop the vehicle.

b) Keep driving until you reach a service station.

c) Hold the steering wheel firmly and keep the vehicle straight while slowing down.

d) Swerve to the side of the road to avoid other vehicles.

21. High-Occupancy Vehicle (HOV) lanes are reserved for:

a) Large trucks and commercial vehicles.

b) Motorcycles only.

c) Vehicles carrying two or more people.

d) Electric and hybrid vehicles.

22. A center lane between lanes of traffic traveling in opposite directions may be designated for:

a) Overtaking slow-moving vehicles.

b) Emergency parking.

c) Left turns by vehicles from both directions.

d) Right turns by vehicles from both directions.

23. If you plan to turn beyond an intersection, you must:

a) Use the left lane.

b) Signal after you pass through the intersection.

c) Signal just before you turn.

d) Use the right lane.

24. When parking on a public road, you must park parallel to and within ____ inches of the curb or edge of the roadway.

a) 12 inches.

b) 18 inches.

c) 24 inches.

d) 36 inches.

25. What should you do if another driver tailgates your vehicle?

a) Increase your speed to create more distance.

b) Brake suddenly to warn the driver.

c) Pull over to the side of the road and let the driver pass.

d) Use hand gestures to signal the driver to back off.

26. What does this sign mean?

[Image: A sign with a picture of a gas pump]

a) Gas station ahead.

b) No gas stations for the next 50 miles.

c) Environmental conservation area.

d) Construction zone ahead.


27. When should you switch on your high-beam headlights?

a) In foggy conditions.

b) When driving in heavy traffic.

c) When following another vehicle closely.

d) When driving in dark rural areas without streetlights.

28. When turning left from a multi-lane one-way road onto another one-way road, start your turn from:

a) The left-most lane.

b) The right-most lane.

c) Any lane you prefer.

d) The center lane.

**Short Answers Key:**

| 1. a) | 2. b) |
|---|---|
| 3. c) | 4. d) |
| 5. d) | 6. b) |
| 7. a) | 8. b) |
| 9. d) | 10. c) |
| 11. c) | 12. a) |
| 13. a) | 14. b) |
| 15. d) | 16. d) |
| 17. c) | 18. d) |
| 19. b) | 20. c) |
| 21. c) | 22. c) |
| 23. c) | 24. b) |
| 25. c) | 26. a) |
| 27. d) | 28. a) |

## Quizz 4
1. Which of the following statements about passing other vehicles is true?

a) It is safe to pass on the right side of the vehicle in front of you.

b) Passing is allowed in no passing zones if you can do it quickly.

c) Always check for oncoming traffic and use your turn signals before passing.

d) Passing is prohibited on highways but allowed on residential streets.

2. Which of the following statements about using headlights is FALSE?

a) You should use your headlights during adverse weather conditions.

b) High beams should be used when driving in well-lit urban areas.

c) Use low beams when following another vehicle closely.

d) Headlights should be used half an hour before sunrise and half an hour after sunset.

3. Following too closely behind another vehicle is called:

a) Tailgating.

b) Drafting.

c) Hugging.

d) Stalking.

4. You are driving on the freeway and notice another driver using a handheld cell phone. What is the best thing to do?

a) Ignore the situation as it is not your concern.

b) Honk your horn to alert the driver about the danger.

c) Report the incident to the appropriate authorities if possible.

d) Take a picture of the driver using the phone as evidence.

5. When you turn left from a one-way street onto another one-way street, you should turn into:

a) Any available lane.

b) The rightmost lane.

c) The leftmost lane.

d) The center lane.

6. Large electronic flashing arrow panels may be used in work zones day and night to:

a) Display traffic messages and signals to drivers.

b) Provide directions to nearby gas stations.

c) Indicate the presence of wildlife on the road.

d) Warn drivers about sharp curves ahead.

7. At an intersection, you should yield to another vehicle:

a) Only if it is a large commercial truck.

b) Coming from the left if you arrived at the intersection simultaneously.

c) Coming from the right if you arrived at the intersection simultaneously.

d) If it is an emergency vehicle with its lights and siren activated.

8. The wide white line painted across a traffic lane before an intersection is known as a:

a) Stop line.

b) Crosswalk line.

c) Merge line.

d) Centerline.

9. What does this sign mean?

a) Bicycle lane ends.

b) Bicycles not allowed on this road.

c) Watch for bicycles crossing the road.

d) Bike rental station nearby.

10. What should you do if you are overtaking a bicycle and an oncoming vehicle is approaching at the same time?

a) Honk your horn to alert the oncoming vehicle.

b) Continue overtaking the bicycle and force the oncoming vehicle to yield.

c) Slow down and let the oncoming vehicle pass before overtaking the bicycle.

d) Speed up and complete the overtaking maneuver quickly.

11. If a car approaches you with its high-beam headlights on, you must _____ to keep yourself from being temporarily blinded.

a) Turn on your high beams in response.

b) Flash your headlights multiple times.

c) Look to the right side of the road.

d) Look to the left side of the road.

12. Lanes of traffic going in opposite directions are divided by:

a) Solid white lines.

b) Broken yellow lines.

c) Double solid yellow lines.

d) Double white lines.

13. On a highway with three or more lanes going in one direction, vehicles passing others or turning left should use:

a) The leftmost lane.

b) The rightmost lane.

c) The center lane.

d) Any lane that is available.

**Answer Key:**

| 1. c)  | 2. b)  |
|--------|--------|
| 3. a)  | 4. c)  |
| 5. c)  | 6. a)  |
| 7. c)  | 8. a)  |
| 9. c)  | 10. c) |
| 11. c) | 12. b) |
| 13. a) |        |

# Quizz 5

(1) You are required to notify the DMV within a period of five days if you:

(a) vend or convey your vehicle (b) reapply a new coat of paint to it.

(c) Obtain a traffic ticket.

(2) Is it illegal for an individual who is 21 years old or above to operate a vehicle with a blood alcohol concentration (BAC) equal to or exceeding the legal limit?

(a) 0.08%.

(b) 0.10%

c) 0.05%

(3) When transitioning between lanes or incorporating into another lane, you must adhere to the subsequent guidelines:

(a) Possess the privilege of passage

(b) Cease initially to search for approaching vehicles

(c) Permit a minimum of a four-second interval in the flow of vehicles.

(4) Which of the subsequent statements is accurate for drivers and motorbike operators?

a) Motorbike operators are prohibited from travelling at a faster pace than other automobiles on a congested pathway

b) They are bound by the identical statutes and guidelines as other motorists.

c) Motorcycles are less affected as they are more substantial than other forms of vehicles.

(5) You desire to depart a parking spot by reversing. Make sure to consistently retreat and examine:

(a) When you reverse, check your side mirrors

(b) as well as your rearview mirror

(c) While you go back, look over your right and left shoulders.

6. If a vehicle nearing your position has initiated a leftward manoeuvre in your path:

(a) Honk your horn to alert the other vehicle and continue moving

(b) Continue moving and shift towards the right

(c) Decrease speed or apply the brakes to prevent accidents

(7) When parking, rotate your front wheels in the opposite direction:

(A) ascending (B) descending (C) on even terrain

(8) In the absence of any contrary instructions, the subsequent velocity restrictions are applicable in residential and commercial zones:

(a) 25 miles per hour (b) 30 miles per hour (c) 35 miles per hour

(9). It is advisable to exercise greater prudence when driving in or around

a) residential zones, educational institutions, or recreational spaces

b) while overtaking large vehicles

c) desiring to witness a regulated collision.

(10) While operating a vehicle and observing the road ahead, it is important to:
(a) consistently maintain a forward gaze
(b) concentrate solely on the automobiles ahead of you
(c) carefully examine your environment..

**Answers :**
(1)a (2)a (3)c (4)b (5)c (6)c (7)a (8)a (9)a (10)c


(11) A large automobile is navigating through the middle of three lanes. You plan to surpass the large truck. It's more desirable to refuse.

(a) Glide rapidly to the left and ahead of it.

(b) Proceed ahead of it while shifting softly towards the left.

(c) Hastily move to the right and ahead of it.

(12) You are journeying in the lane nearest to the middle partition on a five-lane motorway.

a) You should carefully traverse all lanes simultaneously in order to exit the highway on the correct side.

(b) Switch lanes individually until you are in the accurate lane.

(c) Decelerate prior to initiating each lane alteration.

(13) It is important to consistently be vigilant for motorbike riders prior to making a turn as they need to have an unbroken succession of vehicles, consistently possess the privilege of passage at intersections, and are challenging to perceive because of their diminished size.

(14) It is prohibited to traverse dual unbroken yellow lines situated in the centre of the roadway in order to

(a) Overtake another vehicle

(b) Take a left

(c) Perform a U-turn

(15) A educational institution vehicle has come to a halt and is illuminating its red lights in front on your road. What should you do?

When you believe it is secure to proceed, you ought to:

A. Halt initially.

B. Cease movement when the red lights are flickering.

C. Halt until all the kids have traversed the road.

(16) In the event that you are accused of any of the subsequent transgressions:

(a) Discarding or forsaking an animal on a roadway

(b) Executing a reversal from a middle left-turn

(c) Stationing in a bicycle, you could potentially incur a penalty of up to $1,000 and half a year of incarceration.

(17) In the event of a collision, it is necessary to furnish the subsequent details to the opposing party:

A) Your identification number

B) Evidence of insurance

C) vehicle registration

D) present residence

(18) When operating a vehicle during the evening, utilise your bright lights:

(a) To the minimum extent feasible, solely on pathways lacking illumination.

(c) When it is secure and permissible to proceed.

(19) When is it permissible to utilise a cellular device while operating a vehicle without a hands-free apparatus?

(a) While placing a phone call at a stop signal

(b) or when dialling for assistance in a crisis

(c) It is always advised to refrain from

(20) You should come to a halt near the right border of the street as practicable

(a) yield to the emergency vehicle before transitioning into the right lane

(b) cautiously proceed after it has gone by.

(c) Halting abruptly, without delay, including at a crossroad.

# Answer key:

(11)a (12)b (13)c (14)a (15)b (16)a (17)c (18)c (19)b (20)a

(21) You are observed driving a car while your blood alcohol concentration (BAC) is equal to or surpassing the lawful threshold:

(A) The officials possess the authority to punish you.

(B) The findings of your breathalyser alone cannot be employed to incriminate you.

(C) Irrespective of the type of licence you possess, your driver's licence will be promptly withdrawn.

(22) While at a railway intersection with multiple tracks, only proceed when you have clear visibility in both directions, the locomotive has gone by, or other vehicles have begun to traverse.

(23) Parking is accessible as indicated by this azure sign:

(a) Exclusively for individuals utilising wheelchairs

(b) For individuals with impairments who do not possess a distinct licence plate or sign.

(c) Exclusively for individuals with disabilities who possess a distinctive licence plate or identifier.

(24) The significance of this yellow symbol is as follows: A diamond shape in yellow colour featuring two black arrows indicating opposite directions.

(a) Lanes converge up ahead (b) Dual carriageway up ahead (c) Blocked road up ahead

(25) There exists a solitary lane proceeding in your direction, and frequently the automobile ahead of you unexpectedly decelerates. In this situation, you ought to (a) Speed up to pass the vehicle as swiftly as possible.

(b) Increase the distance between you and the other by the specified quantity:

(c) Swiftly flicker your headlights to alert the other driver.

When manoeuvring around a sharp bend, it is advisable to apply the brakes in order to decrease the speed of your vehicle.

(a) Right before approaching the bend (b) During the entire bend.

You are approaching a junction prior to entering the bend of this sentence (27). The red blinking traffic signal is here. What should you do?

(a) Thoroughly examine the intersection.

(b) Halt prior to entering. (c) Proceed ahead prior to entering. Wait until the signal changes to green.

(28) What is the top recommendation for operating a vehicle in severe mist or particulate matter circumstances?

(a) Attempt to postpone driving until the circumstances improve.

(b) Refrain from driving at a sluggish pace to prevent getting hit by other vehicles.

(c) alternate between dim and bright headlights to improve your vision.

(29) You are journeying along a divided road that contains numerous lanes directing in your direction. Where should you start if a U-turn is required?

(a) in the middle (b) upon the (c) in the far left lane.

(30) Engaging in tobacco use within a vehicle in the presence of an individual below 18 years old is: If it belongs to you, it is either (a) permissible (b) consistently unlawful (c) not expressly forbidden by legislation.

**Answers: (21)c (22)a (23)c (24)b (25)b (26)c (27)b (28)a (29)c (30)b**

(31) What statement regarding other motorists is true?

When employing blinkers, motorists must consistently proceed in the designated path. You must also never presume that other vehicles will yield to you.

(32) It is unlawful to abandon a child in a vehicle without supervision if they are below the age of six:

(A) While the vehicle is in motion

(B) In the event that the child is accompanied by a sibling or male sibling at the age of 12.

C) On a cold, damp day with all the windows shut.

(33) On the intersection, an individual holding a white walking stick is on the verge of traversing the road. The person retreats and retrieves his walking stick. If the individual is unready to traverse the road, you ought to:

(a) Manoeuvre your vehicle across the road

(b) Cease your motorised vehicle a minimum of six feet away from the pedestrian crossing

(c) Sound your horn to indicate to the person to traverse the road.

(34). driving at a slower speed than the flow of the traffic

a. increasing the likelihood of a crash  b. reducing the probability

c. not altering the probability of a crash happening.

(35) At what location should you bring your vehicle to a halt if there is no pedestrian crossing or boundary line?

a. Slightly past corner B at the intersection

(b) 20 feet prior to the corner

36. Which of the subsequent assertions concerning devoted turning lanes governed by a verdant arrow is accurate whilst you are situated within one?

a. All incoming vehicles and walkers are required to halt at the intersection.

(b) Give way to you.

(c) You are permitted to make a turn in the direction indicated by the arrow without initially verifying for any vehicles.

Which of the following roads is more prone to hiding ice patches on chilly, wet days?

(a) Highways close to mountain peaks (b) roadways and elevated structures

(38) Decelerating solely for the purpose of witnessing collisions or any atypical occurrences:

(a) Traffic jam

(b) Averts collisions from behind

(c) Improves the movement of vehicles by preventing collisions

(39) You ought to maintain a broader range of sight on a highway compared to that of an urban road.

(a) To identify potential hazards

(b) Your car requires a distance of one-fourth of a mile to come to a halt.

(c) Since it allows you to sustain the movement of vehicles

(40) In the event that one of the subsequent circumstances transpires:

(a) In the event that you intend to submit a declaration of inactivity for your automobile, it is imperative that you reach out to the authorities.

(a) present a documented account (SR 1) to the Department of Motor Vehicles.

b)Your vehicle is confiscated for parking incorrectly.

(c) You are involved in a collision, and someone sustains injuries or loses their life.

**Answers: (31)c (32)a (33)a (34)b (35)b (36)b (37)b (38)a (39)a (40)c**

(41) It is crucial to inspect the traffic behind you on three specific occasions:

(a) Reversing, executing a sudden curve, or traversing a junction.

(b) Accelerating, switching lanes, or decelerating abruptly.

(c) Switching lanes, traversing intersections, or decelerating

(42) The presence of this particular white sign indicates the prohibition of overtaking: a rectangular shape in white hue, accompanied by a circular shape in red colour and a slanted line traversing it diagonally.

(a) Continue until you surpass the marker

(b) Except if it appears secure to proceed

(c) Different modes of transportation for various purposes

(43) If a curb is painted blue, it indicates that parking is:

(a) Limited to a maximum duration of 15 minutes

(b) Intended solely for the purpose of passenger pick-up or drop-off

(c) Reserved exclusively for individuals with disabilities who possess a designated placard or licence plate.

(44) The yellow lines serve as a division:

(a) The allocation of lanes for traffic on streets that only allow movement in one direction. (b) Vehicles travelling in opposite directions on a road that permits traffic flow in both ways.

(c) The separation of carpool lanes from regular traffic lanes is a common practise. Once you have successfully overtaken a vehicle, it is considered safe to merge back into your original driving lane under the following circumstances:

(a) The driver of the vehicle you passed explicitly indicates that it is safe for you to re-enter your lane.

(b) You clearly communicate your intention to return to your lane by using your turn signal for a duration of three seconds.

(c) You visually confirm the presence of the passed vehicle's headlights in your rearview mirror.

(46) You are allowed to execute a left turn on a red light solely from a:

(a) Entering a two-way road from a single direction

(b) Accessing a single direction road from a single direction

(c) Joining a single direction road from a road with two directions

(47) A vehicle displaying a sign of this particular shape in orange and red always indicates:

(a) The vehicle is granted priority

(b) Traffic is moving at a snail's pace up ahead.

(c) Construction is taking place on the shoulder up ahead.

(48) It is important to be aware of bicycle riders who use the same lanes as motor vehicles due to the following reasons:

(a) They are required to ride in the same direction as traffic flow.

(b) They do not have the legal right to occupy lanes alongside motor vehicles.

(c) They have the privilege to share the road with other vehicles.

(49) When you encounter a traffic light with a red arrow pointing to the right, you have two options:

(a) You can proceed to turn in that direction after ensuring that you slow down and carefully assess the traffic situation. (

b) Alternatively, you must refrain from making any turns in that direction until the traffic light changes to green.

(c) Make a right turn once you have fully halted.

50. A person on foot initiates their journey across the road once the "Do Not Proceed" indicator commences its intermittent illumination. As soon as your traffic light turns green, you notice a pedestrian standing right in the middle of the road. You must:

(a) Continue if you are legally allowed to do so

(b) Continue if there are no pedestrians in your designated area

(c) Wait until the pedestrian has safely crossed the road before proceeding.

Answers: (41)b  (42)c  (43)c  (44)b  (45)c  (46)b  (47)c  (48)c  (49)b  (50)c

# Evaluate your progress and identify areas for improvement

To evaluate your progress and identify areas for improvement for the California DMV exam, you can follow these steps:

**Take Practice Tests:** Start by taking practice tests that simulate the real exam. Many online platforms offer DMV practice tests for California. These tests will help you assess your knowledge of the rules, regulations, and traffic signs.

**Review the DMV Handbook:** Read the California DMV Driver Handbook thoroughly. Pay close attention to topics you find challenging or need clarification on.

**Analyze Practice Test Results:** After completing each practice test, review your results. Identify the questions you got wrong and understand why you made those mistakes.

**Focus on Weak Areas:** Based on the mistakes you made in the practice tests, focus on studying the topics and rules that you find difficult. Spend more time reviewing those areas.

**Seek Additional Resources:** If you're still having trouble with certain topics, consider using other resources like online tutorials, videos, or study guides to reinforce your understanding.

**Take More Practice Tests:** Once you've studied and reviewed weak areas, take more practice tests to gauge your improvement. Aim for consistent scores and ensure you're comfortable with the material.

**Time Management:** During the practice tests, pay attention to the time it takes you to complete each test. The real exam is time-limited, so practice managing your time effectively.

**Stay Calm and Confident:** As the exam day approaches, stay calm and confident in your preparation. Believe in yourself and your abilities.

## Prepare for the exam day:

**Get Adequate Rest:** Make sure you get enough sleep the night before the exam to be well-rested and alert.

**Eat a Healthy Meal:** Have a balanced and nutritious meal before the exam to keep your energy levels up.

**Arrive Early:** Plan to arrive at the DMV test center early to avoid unnecessary stress and last-minute rushes.

**Bring Required Documents:** Ensure you have all the necessary identification and paperwork required for the exam.

**Stay Positive:** Maintain a positive mindset and visualize yourself passing the exam successfully.

**Read Questions Carefully:** During the exam, read each question carefully and take your time to choose the correct answer.

**Eliminate Wrong Choices:** If you're unsure about an answer, try to eliminate obviously wrong choices to narrow down your options.

**Focus on Traffic Signs:** Pay close attention to traffic signs and their meanings. Many questions on the exam are related to traffic signs.

**Relax and Breathe:** If you feel nervous, take a deep breath and relax. Trust in your preparation and take the test with confidence.

Remember, passing the California DMV exam requires preparation, focus, and a calm demeanor. Good luck!

# Conclusion

## Congratulations, you're ready for the DMV exam!

Congratulations on becoming DMV exam ready! You've worked hard to prepare for this critical stage by studying, exercising, and practicing. Remember to maintain your composure and attention during the test and believe in the information you have learned.

To guarantee a good test day, remember these last-minute tips:

**Take a deep breath and maintain your composure.** Try to be calm and collected since anxiety might impair your performance.

**Carefully read:** Close attention to significant information by thoroughly reading each question. Take your time answering the questions.

**Answer with assurance:** Believe in your preparedness and respond with confidence. Make your most informed estimate in response to an uncertain question.

**Observe Your Time:** Watch the clock and pace yourself appropriately. Avoid focusing too much time on a single question.

**Review Your Answers:** If you complete the exam before the allotted time, take a minute to go over your responses. Make sure you didn't commit any obvious errors.

**Follow Directions:** Pay close attention to any directions the test proctor provides.

**Visualize Success:** Envision yourself easily completing the test. Thinking positively may influence events.

**Don't Overthink:** Sometimes, the first solution that pops into your head is the best. Don't second-guess your decisions.

**Drink water :** Drink water before the test to keep hydrated and concentrate.

**Have confidence in yourself.** You've studied hard, and you can pass this test. Have faith in your skills and talents.

Wishing you success on your DMV test! You can do this.

# Additional California Driving Safety and Information Resources

Best wishes for your forthcoming DMV test! Here are some extra sites you may look into to deepen your driving education and keep safe on the road:

**California Driver Handbook:** The DMV's California Driver Handbook is a valuable tool. It contains all California-specific laws, ordinances, and safe driving practices. The manual is available on the DMV's official website.

**Practice Exams:** Keep taking practice exams to solidify your knowledge of traffic regulations, road signs, and safe driving procedures. Many websites provide free California DMV practice exams.

**Online classes:** You may sign up for traffic school or defensive driving classes online. These classes may help you develop your abilities, learn more sophisticated driving tactics, and they can even result in insurance reductions.

**DMV Website:** For updates, significant announcements, and more materials about driving in California, often check the official DMV website.

**Website of the California Highway Patrol (CHP):** The CHP website provides useful information on traffic rules, road safety, and driving advice. It's a fantastic tool for keeping current on traffic safety. Consider enrolling in a local driving school to get hands-on driving instruction. Professional teachers may provide practical advice and insightful observations.

**Applications for Safe Driving:** Look into applications for safe driving that include features like speed limit reminders, real-time traffic information, and notifications for potential dangers on the road. American Automobile Association (AAA) members get discounts on driving-related services and access to resources, instructional materials, and other benefits.

**Community Workshops:** Keep a look out for local traffic safety groups, police stations, or community centers that are hosting workshops or lectures on safe driving.

Peer dialogues are a great way to learn from other's experiences and get helpful advice. Have conversations with seasoned drivers, family members, or friends.

Remember that driving is a skill that must be continually learned and improved. Keep yourself educated, drive carefully, and always prioritize others and your safety. Wishing you success on your test and a lot of safe and fun driving in California in the future!

# Appendix

## Glossary of driving terminology

To help you better comprehend the numerous phrases associated with driving, below is a dictionary of frequently used driving terminology:

**Acceleration:** Increasing a vehicle's speed via acceleration.

**Blind spot :** The area of a car that cannot be seen clearly in the driver's side mirrors is called the blind spot.

**Braking distance:** The distance a car travels after applying the brakes until it reaches a full stop is known as the braking distance.

**Crosswalk:** A designated location for pedestrians to cross the street.

**Defensive driving: This** is a safe technique that entails foreseeing possible dangers and taking proactive steps to prevent collisions.

**Distracted driving** occurs when a driver does anything that takes their focus off the road, including talking on a phone, eating, or fiddling with the radio.

**DUI/DWI:** Operating a vehicle while intoxicated or under the influence of drugs is known as driving under the influence (DUI) or driving while intoxicated (DWI).

**Freeway:** A split, high-speed road without junctions or traffic lights.

**Highway:** A major thoroughfare linking villages and cities.

**Lane:** A lane is a segment of the road that is set aside for vehicular traffic.

**Merge**: A seamless transition from two lanes of traffic to one.

**Overtaking:** Overtaking is the act of passing another moving object in the same direction.

**Parallel parking:** Parallel parking refers to putting a car in a side-by-side parking position with the curb.

**Right of Way:** The ability to go forward first in a line of traffic or at a crosswalk.

**Speed Limit**: The maximum speed for vehicles to drive on a certain road.

**Tailgating:** Tailgating is following another vehicle excessively closely and giving yourself little time to respond to abrupt developments.

**U-turn:** Completely turning your car around and moving in the other direction.

**Yield:** To move aside and let pedestrians or other traffic go ahead of you at a junction or specific location.

**Roundabout:** A circular crossroads with a center island where traffic moves in one direction.

**Yellow light:** A yellow light tells cars to be ready to stop before the light turns red.

### Behind-the-wheel
Test of behind-the-wheel driving evaluation in which you are given control of the car and are accompanied by a DMV examiner.

**(BAC) Blood alcohol content:**
The level of alcohol in your blood is known as your BAC. For instance, if your BAC is 0.10 percent, you have 0.10 grams of alcohol in every 100 milliliters of blood.

**Evaluation of driving performance (DPE) :** Driving Performance Evaluation (DPE) is part of the behind-the-wheel drive test when you drive your automobile. At the same time, a DMV examiner assesses your driving abilities.

**Pedestrian:**
A person with a handicap who travels by tricycle, quadricycle, or wheelchair may also be considered a pedestrian.

**Right-of-way** assists in deciding who has the right of way when cars, bicycles, and pedestrians cross paths on the road.

**Rule of three seconds:**
The rule of three seconds is the road safety principle for determining how closely you should follow other cars. Count three seconds after the vehicle in front of you passes a certain location, like a sign. You need to follow more closely if you cross the same place before you have finished counting.

**Traffic ticket:** A traffic citation, sometimes called a token, is a formal summons issued by law enforcement for breaking a traffic law.

**VRUs (vulnerable road users):**
VRUs are non-motorized road users, including bicycles, walkers, and people in wheelchairs, tricycles, and quadricycles with limited mobility or orientation.

# Road sign summary cards

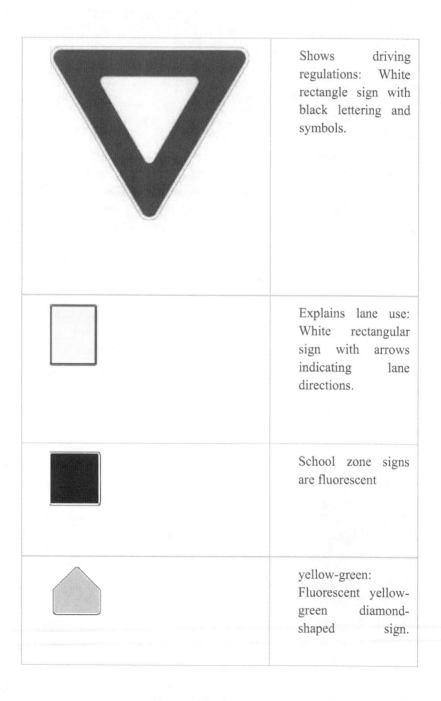

|  |  |
|---|---|
| ■ | Tells about motorist services: Blue rectangle sign with white lettering and symbols. |
| ○ | Shows permitted action: White circular sign with a green border. |
| ⊘ | Shows an action that is not permitted: White circular sign with a red border and a slash over the symbol. |
| ◆ | Warns of hazards ahead: Yellow diamond-shaped sign with black symbols. |

| | |
|---|---|
| ◆ | Warns of construction zones: Orange diamond-shaped sign with black symbols. |
| ✕ | Railway crossing: Round yellow sign with a black "X" and two "RxR" symbols. |
| ▬ | Shows distance and direction: Green rectangular sign with white lettering and symbols. |
| MAXIMUM 70 km/h | The fastest you may drive in good conditions: White rectangular sign with black lettering indicating speed limit. |
| ↑ 50 km/h | Indicates a lower speed limit ahead: White rectangular sign with black lettering indicating upcoming reduced speed limit. |

| | |
|---|---|
| | Do not enter: Red circular sign with a white horizontal bar. |
| | Do not go this way - usually mounted on exit ramps: Red rectangular sign with white lettering and an arrow pointing left. |
| | One way - gives direction of traffic on the cross street: White rectangular sign with black lettering and an arrow pointing in the specified direction. |
| | Winter tires or chains must be used when the sign is displayed: White circular sign with a blue snowflake symbol |

| | |
|---|---|
| [DISASTER RESPONSE ROUTE - EMERGENCY VEHICLES ONLY DURING A DISASTER sign] | Stay off the road during major disasters - the road may be used only by emergency vehicles: White rectangular sign with black lettering and symbols. |
| [SLOWER TRAFFIC KEEP RIGHT sign] | Move into the right lane if driving slower than traffic: White rectangular sign with black lettering and an arrow pointing right. |
| [KEEP RIGHT EXCEPT TO PASS sign] | Keep right unless passing: White rectangular sign with black lettering and an arrow pointing right. |
| [No stopping sign] | No stopping between here and the next no stopping sign: Red circular sign with a white horizontal bar and the word "STOPPING" below. |

| | |
|---|---|
| | No stopping during posted times between here and the next sign: Red circular sign with a white horizontal bar and the word "STOPPING" below, along with a timetable. |
| | No bicycle riding beyond this point: White rectangular sign with a black bicycle symbol and the word "BICYCLES" below. |
| | No right turn on a red light: Red circular sign with a white horizontal bar and the words "NO RIGHT TURN ON RED |
| | Pedestrian activated crosswalk - prepare to stop if the light is flashing: White rectangular sign with a black pedestrian symbol and the words "PEDESTRIAN CROSSING" below. |

| | |
|---|---|
| | Playground nearby - Yellow diamond shape with child figures playing. |
| | Playground zone - White rectangle with black text "30 km/h" and a picture of a child playing. |
| | School zone - White rectangle with black text "50 km/h" and a picture of a school building and clock indicating 8 am to 5 pm. |
| | Turn left only - White rectangle with black arrow pointing left. |
| | Continue straight only - White rectangle with black arrow pointing straight. |
| | Go through or turn left - White rectangle with black arrow pointing straight and another |

|  |  |
|---|---|
|  | arrow pointing left. |
| | Go through or turn right - White rectangle with black arrow pointing straight and another arrow pointing right. |
| | Vehicles from both lanes must turn left, no through traffic allowed - White rectangle with black text "Left turn only" and an arrow pointing left. |
| | Vehicles in both lanes must turn left - White rectangle with black arrow pointing left on a yellow background. |
| | Left turn only - White rectangle with black arrow pointing left on a red background. |
| | Go straight only - White rectangle with black arrow pointing straight on a red background. |

| | |
|---|---|
| | Turn right or left only - White rectangle with black arrows pointing right and left on a red background. |
| | No right turns during posted times - White rectangle with black text "No right turn" and a clock indicating the restricted times. |
| | Time-limited parking during posted times - White rectangle with black text "Time-limited parking" and a clock indicating the restricted times. |
| | Do not park here - Red circle with a diagonal line across a black "P" (parking) symbol. |
| | Parking is not allowed during posted times - White rectangle with black text "No parking" and a clock indicating the restricted times. |

| | |
|---|---|
| | Parking only for vehicles displaying a disabled sign and a person with disabilities - White rectangle with a blue wheelchair symbol. |
| | Only buses in this lane - White rectangle with black text "Bus lane" and a bus symbol. |
| | Only buses and HOV's in this lane - White rectangle with black text "Bus/HOV lane" and a bus and carpool symbol. |
| | Curb lane of cross street ahead is reserved lane - White rectangle with black text "Reserved lane" and an arrow indicating the curb lane. |
| | Winding road ahead - Yellow diamond shape with a squiggly arrow indicating a winding road. |

| | |
|---|---|
| | Hidden side road ahead - Yellow diamond shape with an arrow indicating a side road. |
| | Sharp curve ahead - Yellow diamond shape with an arrow indicating a sharp curve and a suggested speed limit. |
| | Curve ahead - Yellow diamond shape with an arrow indicating a curve. |
| | Merging traffic ahead - Yellow diamond shape with arrows merging. |
| | Road merges with another road - Added lane to the right ahead - White rectangle with black text "Added lane" and an arrow indicating the merging road. |
| | Divided highway ends ahead- keep right: Yellow diamond, two arrows pointing |

| | |
|---|---|
| | right. |
| | Two way traffic ahead: Yellow diamond, two opposing arrows. |
| | Road narrows ahead: Yellow diamond, tapering inward arrows. |
| | Narrow structure ahead- often a bridge: Yellow diamond, narrow structure icon. |
| | Bump or rough road ahead: Yellow diamond, wavy road icon. |
| | Road may be slippery ahead: Yellow diamond, wavy lines icon. |
| | Stop sign ahead: Red octagon, "STOP" in white. |
| | Roundabout ahead: White circle, arrows indicating a roundabout. |

| | |
|---|---|
| | Signal lights ahead: Yellow diamond, traffic signals icon. |
| | Signal lights ahead- prepare to stop when lights are flashing: Yellow diamond, traffic signals with additional text. |
| | Detour ahead: Yellow diamond, "DETOUR" in black. |
| | Soft shoulder ahead- stay off: Yellow diamond, soft shoulder icon with text. |
| | Construction ahead: Orange diamond, construction symbol. |
| | Traffic control person ahead: Orange diamond, figure directing traffic. |

| | |
|---|---|
| MAXIMUM 50 km/h | Crew working- obey posted speed limit: Orange diamond, figures working with text. |
| MAXIMUM 70 km/h | Survey crew- obey posted speed limit: Orange diamond, figures surveying with text. |
| Thank you RESUME SPEED | End of construction zone speed limit: Orange rectangle, end of construction zone speed limit sign. |
| ⬅···➡ | Follow the lighted arrow: White rectangle, arrow outlined with lights. |
| BLASTING ZONE SHUT OFF YOUR RADIO TRANSMITTER | Blasting zone- follow instructions on sign: Orange diamond, blasting zone symbol with text. |

| | |
|---|---|
| Kelowna 53<br>Penticton 116 | Destination sign- distances are in kilometres: Green rectangle, destination distances in kilometers. |
| ↑ Coquitlam<br>← Port Moody<br>Maple Ridge → | Directional sign: Green rectangle, arrows pointing in various directions. |
| (Trans-Canada shield with maple leaf) | Trans-Canada highway route marker: White rectangle with a red maple leaf and the Trans-Canada Highway logo. |
| 99 B.C. | Primary highway marker sign: White rectangle with the highway number in black. |
| H | Hospital nearby: White rectangle with an "H" and a red cross. |
| (gas pump icon) | Gas available ahead: White rectangle with a gas pump icon and text. |

| | |
|---|---|
| | Accommodation ahead: White rectangle with a bed icon and text. |
| | Travel information ahead: White rectangle with an "i" (information) icon and text. |

# Notes and space for personal annotations

_____
_____
_____
_____
_____
_____
_____
_____
_____
_____
_____
_____
_____
_____
_____
_____
_____
_____

Made in the USA
Las Vegas, NV
06 November 2023

80358249R00066